Predictions of the Prophets Why Has Jesus Not Returned?

A Shocking New Theory

Stanley J. St. Clair, B.R.E., A.S.L., K.T.J.

Foreward by
Jacqueline De Berry, D.Min., M.Div., B.S.

Original Manuscript Edited by
Genevieve Abalos, A.S.W

Final Manuscript Professionally Edited by
Michele Doucette, M. Ed.

Predictions of the Prophets: Why Has Jesus Not Returned?

ISBN 978-1-947514-15-7

Printed in the United States of America and the UK

St. Clair Publications
P. O. Box 726
Mc Minnville, TN 37111—0726

http://stclairpublications.com

Cover Design by Kent Grey—Hesselbein Design Studio

www.kghdesignstudio.com

Table of Contents

The ideas contained in this work are not necessarily those of my family, my friends, other associates of St. Clair Publications, or any particular religious group, association or organization, but were developed solely by the research and study of the author.

———————————◆✕◆———————————

All Scripture used herein is taken from the King James Version of the Bible except those noted to be from the English translation of the Hebrew Tanakh, or the NIV.

This book is lovingly dedicated to the memory of my dear father, Marvin Woodrow St. Clair (3-15-1919 – 10-6-1980) on the occasion of the 100th anniversary of his birth. A good and honorable man, who sacrificed much for the good of his family, he was an avid student of the Holy Scriptures, and a loving father. Taken far too soon, he continues to live on in my memory, with the fondest hope of a reunion in the next life.

In 2007, after having completed my manuscript for *Prayers of Prophets, Knights and Kings* the year before (Trafford Publishing, Victoria, BC, Canada. 2006), I felt that I had thrown out a lot of comparative religious information, with very little of my own feelings.

My roots were deep in the religious fervor of the Bible Belt in the Southern United States. I was brought up in a home which had solid faith in Christ and Christian values. As a youth I had felt called to the service of God, and attended college and seminary, spending a time in mission work, and had a weekly program called *The Gospel of the Kingdom* on three radio stations simultaneously in the early 1970s, one of which was a powerful FM station in Chattanooga. Troubled marriage and divorce took me away from this, and kept me wondering if I had chosen correctly. I built a career in insurance marketing, but I completed my degree in Religious Education, retained my faith, and remained active in church and teaching ministry.

Involvement in, and study of various Christian doctrines taught me that though there were many views of the Scripture, each group felt that their belief was the right one. This bothered me, especially with those who saw theirs as the only true way.

Comparative religion became a hot topic with me, and I made it my business to know how a group believed, and why. A touchy subject for me has long been eschatology, from the Greek ἔσχατον (éskhaton), meaning last, plus *logy*, the doctrine of final things.

When I became involved with the Clan Sinclair Association in 2001, I did so with the desire to discover who these people were, and was very skeptical of their intent. I had read negative reports about the Sinclairs, and the Knights Templar, with whom they are often associated.

As time went on, I became engrossed with the entire Scottish scene, and the genuine pleasure that the clans derived from the preservation of their heritage. I began to find a variety of reasons that people become involved in genealogy; some, the music, and many, the fascinating history of their family.

After accepting a post as Commissioner, I became personally acquainted with the international leaders, such as Lord Malcolm, Earl of Caithness, and his relative, Niven Sinclair, Esq., a highly successful London businessman, now deceased, who had been interviewed on several television specials in relation to the speculations raised in Dan Brown's runaway best-seller, *The Da Vinci Code*, which was brought to the big screen in May, 2006 by Ron Howard, and starred Tom Hanks.

In early 2005, because of the Sinclair/St. Clair DNA Project which I was just pioneering with my distant cousin, Steve St. Clair, a New York Ad Executive (who was later a regular guest on the TV show, *America Unearthed*, hosted by Scott Wolter, who had also become a friend of mine as well after meeting him in a conference in Halifax, Nova Scotia), I was contacted by the National Geographic Channel for a possible interview for Spencer Wells' series, *Search for Adam*, on a segment to be titled, *DNA Mysteries*. For various reasons, the segment was cut, and was never filmed.

In 2003, after careful research, I had agreed to be knighted by the *Sovereign Military Order of the Temple at Jerusalem*, a modern ecumenical Christian fraternity of the *Knights Templar*, not affiliated with the Freemasons. For personal reasons, I have remained inactive in the activities of the Order.

One of the primary reasons for my involvement with the Clan Sinclair Association was the aspect of genealogy. In my research, I have found that without a doubt, I have several lines which lead back to the royal houses of Europe.

My circle of personal friends and contacts continued to mushroom, including numerous researchers, world-renowned scientists, authors, politicians in the upper echelon of various countries, professors, Native American first family leaders, and high-ranking members of "secret societies."

I read diverse books, and watched various television specials, concerning Jesus' possible marriage to Mary Magdalene, and the dynasty said to have sprung from them. Works such as Margaret Starbird's *The Woman with the Alabaster Jar: Mary Magdalen and the Holy Grail* (ISBN 1-879181-03-7, Bear and Co., 1993), offered compelling arguments. Strangely enough, the sources are at odds as to whether the "holy family" had one or more children, and even vary as to the name, or names they were to have been given. If these stories are true, I would be a descendant of this lineage through lines other than my direct male ancestry. This claim was frightening to me. The implications of this doctrine seemed to lead to predictions of the world leader known in Christian teachings as 'the Anti-Christ.' I became so connected to those promoting this viewpoint that I even wrote an article for the British publication, *The Temple*. Whether intentional or not, when it was published, my wording was slightly altered to make it seem that I was in 100% agreement with the belief.

As a result of my keen interest in eschatology, and in prophetic writings in general, I began to delve very deeply into these prophecies. Many of the ideas which I came to believe to be credible are not new, but I developed a fresh theory, which to my knowledge, has never, before or since the writing of my original manuscript, been declared. Not feeling that the final result of my work was something which I could comfortably reveal at that time, I shelved it and re-invented myself as an author, doing about ten years of research of the expressions used in everyday English and their origins. This effort, *Most Comprehensive Origins of Clichés, Proverbs and Figurative Expressions*, was highly successful, garnering much praise from those in the know of the topic.

I recently pulled my prophecy manuscript out and allowed my pastor, Rev. Dr. Jacqueline De Berry, to read it. She felt that it was time to put it before the world. The final result is recorded in this book, originally written by me in 2007. I have left that text as much intact as possible, adding only applicable updates, aided by the sharp insight of my pastor. The scenario builds to a climactic conclusion.

Prepare to be shocked.

Foreword: Rev. Dr. Jacqueline De Berry

It is true that history often repeats itself. It is also true that, throughout the ages, people have wondered and attempted to understand eschatological writings, the Parousia, and Apocalyptic literature only to be frustrated. Most people allow these topics of extreme importance to settle somewhere within themselves and their interest in such quietly fades away. They give up the study. Folks who, at one time, burned with a passion to understand such matters, often allow questions and disagreements about theology to cause a fire, ignited by the Holy Ghost to turn into a fading ember. They closed the books and said, "It is too hard." I am so thankful that Stan St. Clair has not done that.

In the past few decades, I have often stated, "We live in a time unlike any other. We live in a time of convergence." By that I mean multiple events are happening at record breaking speed. Biblical prophecies are being fulfilled at a fast rate. For years, I have studied such matters, written about them, preached and taught them. One has to be able to tie matters of today to Biblical prophecy to see the big picture. It has been my experience that few people know how to do this.

There is a big picture and few get it. Stan St. Clair gets it!

While I am not a date prognosticator, nor do I find our author attempting to do such, he does bring forth a novel interpretation of Biblical times and seasons. As he repeats the Biblical mandate to, "Watch and be sober," he has done precisely that. Jesus encourages us to know the seasons of our times. "Now learn a lesson from the fig tree, when its buds become tender and its leaves begin to sprout, you know without being told that summer is near. Just so, when you see the events I've described beginning to happen, you can know His return is very near, right at the door." (Matthew 24: 32-33) He continues in the 44th verse, "You also must be ready all the time. For the Son of Man will come when least expected."

We are to be prepared and to understand such matters. These statements by Jesus are not a license to forget about the matter. We are to know the season.

Few Christians understand the Scriptures in light of a Jewish mindset. The Scriptures reveal a Jewish King and Messiah. The Bible comes to us from the Jews. It is imperative that we understand our history in its context if we are going to be able to make sense out of our Lord's words. Few Christians understand that the Christian account of Jesus' time in the tomb before His resurrection doesn't line up with scripture. We have our Good Friday service and proclaim that He was buried on Friday. Friday evening is the beginning of the Sabbath. Then we celebrate His resurrection on Sunday morning. The Jews have the correct time frame as Stan St. Clair explains it.

I've often thought of writing a book about the "Convergence" of events and times, knowing that it would be a huge undertaking. Stan St. Clair has done precisely that. His understanding of the various disciplines involved in his work shows that he has indeed, 'studied to show himself as a workman who need not be ashamed.' His works represents a vast knowledge of history, Judaism, Christianity, other religions, current events, all presented with sound theology.

His approach is different and his conclusions are unique as well as novel. They are worth the time and reflection of any serious student of God's word. I am honored to write this foreword and to be Stan St. Clair's pastor.

❖

Rev. Dr. Jacqueline De Berry lives in McMinnville, Tennessee, where she is the pastor of the Liberty Cumberland Presbyterian Church. She holds a B.S. degree, a Master of Divinity Degree, and a Doctorate of Ministry.

Ordained in 1981, her ministry has included being a Pastor, a Spiritual Director, the first woman Editor of *The Cumberland Presbyterian Magazine,* and a Chaplain.

A Board Certified Chaplain, a Board Certified Pastoral Counselor and a Spiritual Director, she is also published writer.

She is the mother of two sons as well as a grandmother. Her deepest desire is to glorify God with her life.

Chapter One

The Basis of My Study

In many religions, not just Christianity and Judaism, 'the end of the world,' or more properly, 'the end of the age' (Greek, *aἰών*, or transliterated, aión), meaning 'cycle of time,' is foretold in their sacred writings. These religions include the Mayans, who predicted earthquakes and natural disasters before the end, which was to occur on December 21, 2012, at which time their supreme god, Kulkulcam, the equivalent to the Aztec Quetzalcoti, was to appear, bringing peace and harmony to earth. The Sioux also believe that floods and earthquakes are a sign of the end, and that in about 1995, a white buffalo was born, who could be the 'White Buffalo Calf Woman' of their prophecy who will purify the world, bringing harmony and spiritual balance. Some say this has already happened. [1] Perhaps the oldest eschatology in recorded history is found in Zoroastrianism, another religion discussed in *Prayers of Prophets, Knights and Kings.* By 500 BC, this religion, which also believes in a final judgment of all souls, had developed the concept of the divine destruction of the world by fire, a belief found in Christianity. [2]

Other religions with eschatological beliefs and prophecies include Buddhism, Hinduism, Islam, and even Norse mythology and Neopaganistic sects.

Judaism predicts a termination of our age, followed by a future led by the *meshi'ahh*, or 'Anointed One,' when the true elect will rule. According to Islam prophet, Mohammed Ali Ibn Zubair Ali, [3] the New Age will come with the arrival of the 'Enlightened One,' Imarm, reminiscent of Buddha, His coming is to be at a time when natural disasters will take place. Rather than being 'caught away,' as is a prevailing Fundamentalist Christian teaching, brought to the forefront by in modern times by the *Left Behind* series of books by Tim Lahaye, and the resultant motion pictures, in Zubair Ali's teachings, all believers will be killed. Only unbelievers are to face the final days, which are much as those "left behind" after the 'rapture.' The angel, Isafil, like the judeo-Christian angel, Gabriel, will then blow a trumpet, and the resurrection of all peoples will take place.

Around the turn of the millennium, one would have to have been 'hiding under a rock,' so to speak, not to have been aware of the great movement being stirred about by varying sects regarding the end of our age, and the heralding of a new one. Although this subject is not being discussed as openly as it was when my original manuscript of this book was written, it is being discussed freely in Gnostic realms, something which I have kept open in order to be abreast of actual events which will herald the unmistakable open advent of the 'New Age.'

New Age music would begin in the late 1960s and early seventies with such artists as the Fifth Dimension, with their 1969 number one hit, *Aquarius (Let the Sun Shine In)*, and in 1971, former Beatle, John Lennon, with *Imagine*, the true theme song of the New Age, which envisioned a godless society living for the moment, and the world becoming 'one.' This song is still played on 'soft rock' or 'adult contemporary' stations which portray themselves as 'family oriented' with some regularity after over four decades, while many other popular songs of that era are ignored. That same year, fellow Beatle, George Harrison, had a hit with *My Sweet Lord* which chanted praises to Lord Vishnu, the prevailing god of Hinduism. This music gave a new generation the glimpse of a future world, quite changed, in which Christianity would play no part.

Aside from the obvious immediate expectations of the early New Testament Church, prophetic movements began arising in Christianity as early as 1843, when William Miller made the first of several predictions that the world would end in only a few months. [4] Miller was the predecessor of what would become the Seventh Day Adventist Church, Since that time, many others would make similar predictions, all to end up being mocked by those who were skeptics of their prophecies.

In August 2004, the BBC did a series of broadcasts called *A Brief History of the End of Everything,* featuring Brother Guy Consolmagno, a Jesuit astro-physicist, who "came to religion via science and his wonder of the universe." [5] At the Vatican Observatory in Castel Gandolfo, Italy, he compared cutting edge cosmology with Ancient Chinese, Greek, Buddhist, Medieval and Victorian predictions of the end of everything as we know it. Brother Guy believes that the universe will end, but afterward will begin all over and perhaps last forever.

As I alluded to earlier, toward the end of the last millennium, end-time predictions became numerous. It seemed that the time tables were coinciding in various faiths and date-setting was not uncommon.

The website religioustolerance.org, maintained by B.A. Robinson in Ontario, Canada, a site still in operation, keeps abreast of changing religious teachings. In 2007 it listed twenty-three failed end-time predictions for 1998 alone. Even psychics were adamant in their belief in end-time events taking place that particular year.

Madame Verdue, spokesperson for the International Association of Psychics, stated that 92% of their 120,000 members had experienced an end-time vision. [6] During this time, the predictions of French psychic astronomer Michel de Nostradamus were rehashed. He correctly prophesied, it is said, such vital historic events as the death of Henry II of France, even sending him warnings which were unheeded; the London fire of 1666; and the French Revolution. Nostradamus predicted a trio of powerful world leaders, whom he termed "three antichrists," which would be manifest, bringing terror upon the earth. Napoleon Bonaparte was thought to have met the qualifications to have been the first of these. Nostradamus also predicted a final war at the end of our age. [7] Some saw Hitler in this light. He was one of several dominate conquerors in possession of the infamous "Spear of Destiny," aka the Spear of Longinus, said to be the instrument used to pierce the side of Jesus at his crucifixion.

According to legend the Spear had passed through the hands of Constantine, Charlemagne, and the Hapsburg Emperors. [8] It was claimed that whoever possessed the Spear would rule the world. After a colorful history of the lance thought to be this relic, it was transported from Prague to Nuremberg in the spring of 1424, where it remained until 1806. When Napoleon's army approached Nuremberg in the spring of 1796, it was greatly feared that they would seize the Spear and that Bonaparte would rule the world. [9] The legends of the Spear remain alive today; mingled with those of the Holy Grail, they may well play a part in the events leading to the end of our age.

One Internet website, *Rapture Ready*, still lists 60 failed predictions of dates for Christ's return and the end of the world beginning in 53 AD and ending up in 2012. [10] Though most of these prophesied that the end would occur in the 19th or latter 20th centuries, the year 1000 was among that number because of the change of the millennium. All phases of society, states the site, seemed affected by this prediction.

The site's author, Todd Strandberg, also notes that Sir Isaac Newton, Britain's greatest scientist, spent 50 years and wrote 4,500 pages trying to predict when the end of the world was coming. Then he scribbled his conclusion on a scrap of paper, "2060."

A book was written by Edgar Whisenant titled *88 Reasons Why the Rapture is in 1988* (World Bible Society, Nashville, TN, 1988), which became a best-seller. It predicted the date of Christ's return as September **11**[th] through **13**[th] (ironically **9-11** came up exactly **13** years later when the World Trade Center's twin towers were taken down by terrorists' planes). Entire churches were caught up in the fervor of Whisenant's prediction. Though taunting was small when it failed to transpire, it seemed unbelievable that the same author would come out with a new book stating the 'reason' for his error, predicting the next year as the proper time.

One prevailing reason for common beliefs for the end of the world as we know it being around the year 2000 springs from the predictions in the Talmud, the Jewish writings concerning the unwritten laws and chronology of the Jewish people, that the present state of things will only last 6,000 years. [11] According to Jewish tradition, Israelis will return to their homeland (many have already done so), all of their enemies will be defeated, the Temple will be rebuilt in Jerusalem, sacrificial offerings will resume (something I will deal with a bit later), the dead will raise, and the Messiah will appear and be crowned king of Israel. The accepted date of creation in Judaism is said to be either 25 September or 29 March 3760 BCE, based on our modern calendar. Much Fundamentalist Christian belief regarding the end times stems from this premise.

According to present Jewish thought, the year 3006 is equal to their year 5766, except for the variance in the Jewish year beginning in the month of Nisan (March-April), the end of days should occur in 2240. According to Jewish belief, the seventh millennium will be a time of worldwide peace known as Olam Haba (Future World). Many Christian eschatologists see this as a gross error in their calendar, and many Jews have long awaited the Messiah as well, as we have seen from the history of their expectations, and as I shall cover.

Another reason for the common Christian belief in this theory is a combination of prophecies in the Bible pointing to our time. The belief in the seventh millennium being an era of worldwide peace has carried over into Christian teachings. Here, it is simply known as 'The Millennium.' The primary difference is in the identity of the Messiah, Anointed One, or Christ.

In the time of Jesus' life on earth, there was a prevailing attitude that the reign of the Messiah was at hand. Roman oppression was taxing the souls of the Jewish inhabitants of Judea, which was under the puppet king, Herod.

In both the Gospels of Matthew (24:34) and Luke (21:32), Jesus made a startling statement which those who see his ministry as a failure want to use to discredit the prophecies of Christ. In the Matthew account, Jesus had just predicted the destruction of the Temple (*which took place in 70 AD* at the hand of the forces of Titus, when Jerusalem fell to Roman rule). While seated on the Mount of Olives, his disciples asked him what the sign of his coming and 'the end of the world' would be. It is certain that the disciples, at that moment, did not understand about his death, nor that his kingdom would not begin in their generation. Following a long discourse in which he foretold these signs, he said: "...this generation shall not pass till all these things be fulfilled." What did he mean? It is evident that the generation in which he was living has long since passed. Was Jesus mistaken?

It is easy to explain his statement made earlier in the gospel attributed to Matthew, in which he said, "There be some standing here, which shall not see death, till they see the Son of man coming in his kingdom." [12] The gospel attributed to Mark says it this way: "...till they have seen the kingdom of God come with power." [13] The fulfillment of this symbolic prophecy is found in all three synoptic gospels. [14] It is commonly known as 'the transfiguration.' Six days later, it is recorded, Jesus took Peter, James and John (his inner circle) "up into a high mountain apart. And was transfigured before them; and his face did shine as the sun, and his raiment was white as light." [15] He was then accompanied by Moses and Elijah. The scriptures refer to this as a vision of the glorified Christ.

The twenty-fourth chapter of Matthew's gospel contains the most detailed account of the prediction of Jesus in the entire canon of the Christian Bible. In future chapters, I will analyze these prophecies one by one, in order to be objective.

Chapter Two
_____

The Messiah

In order to understand why we should be concerned about the second coming of Jesus, we must establish the validity of his claim as the true Messiah of the Jews.

The grouping of ancient writings which are called the Old Testament by Christians were first known to Jews as the Tanakh, and were comprised of the Torah, or books of the law, aka, the first five books of Moses; the Nivi'im, or books of the prophets; and the Kethuvim, or the writings. Prophecies considered to be speaking of the Messiah (Hebrew *mashi'ahh*, משיח), or Anointed One, are found in all three sections.

More than 300 prophecies in the Old Testament are seen by Christians to be Messianic predictions which are fulfilled by Jesus. Many of these, such as the teaching that he would be a descendant of both Abraham [1] (a reference to the blessing of everyone on earth through his seed), and Isaac [2] (a reference to kings from the loins of Israel), may seem to be vague, and are listed in the books of Moses, rather than those of prophecy.

Being a descendant of Isaac was also a reference to the Star of Jacob, [3] [4] and a scepter rising out of Israel. This becomes clearer, however, when we see the prophecy concerning his descent from Jesse. In this passage we read, "And there shall come a rod out of the stem of Jesse, and a Branch shall grow out of his roots: And the spirit of the Lord shall rest upon him, the spirit of wisdom and understanding, the spirit of council and might, the spirit of knowledge and the fear of the Lord; And shall make him of quick understanding in the fear of the Lord; and he shall not judge after the sight of his eyes, neither reprove after the hearing of his ears; but with righteousness shall he judge the poor, and reprove with equity the meek of the earth; with the rod of his mouth and with the breath of his lips shall he slay the wicked. And righteousness shall be the girdle of his loins, and faithfulness the girdle of his reigns." (Isaiah 11:1-5) This, and the prediction that he would be of the royal line of David, are accepted as Messianic prophecies. Both Jews and Christians agree on this, but other than the descent from Jesse, the above verses have not yet been fulfilled. Fundamentalist Christians see the reference to not judging "after his own eyes" as a meaning that he receives his authority from the Father.

Other Messianic scriptures viewed by some as prophecies which could be fulfilled in another include: that he would be born in Bethlehem, [5] and that he would be born of a virgin; [6] opponents stating that 'virgin' here means simply, 'young woman.' Those relating to his coming, while the Temple is standing in Jerusalem [7] [8] [9] [10] [11], are thought by many Jews and Christians alike to be prophetic of the rebuilding of the Temple in the 'last days.'

Other scriptures are not so easily put aside, however. In my research; first, I found that there are remarkable prophecies relating to the time of his appearing which would indicate the time of Jesus' first advent and of his death, as well as prophecies indicating that a messenger, sounding for the world like John the Baptist, would announce his arrival. [12] [13] No wonder the apostles left all to follow him.

The prophet Daniel proclaimed:

"Seventy weeks are decreed upon thy people and upon the holy city, to finish the transgression, and to make an end of sin, and to forgive iniquity, and to bring in everlasting righteousness, and to seal vision and prophet, and to anoint the most holy place.

"Know therefore and discern, that from the going forth of the word to restore and build Jerusalem unto one anointed, a prince, shall be seven weeks; and for threescore and two weeks, it shall be build again, with broad place and moat, but in troublous times.

"And after the threescore and two weeks shall an anointed one be cut off and be no more." [14]

I have purposely used the Tanakh for these verses from the ninth chapter of the prophecies of Daniel. Here the precise timing of the death of Jesus was foretold. Although to an extent symbolic, this prophecy checks out as a literal seventy weeks of years. Jews were used to calculating shorter time periods into years, as in the year of Jubilee, the fiftieth year after seven Sabbatical years, when all debts were forgiven, and slaves were set free of their obligations and returned to their families. [15] Take, as an example, the 490 years "from the going forth of the world to restore and build Jerusalem unto one anointed, a prince, shall be seven weeks; and for threescore and two weeks, it shall be built again, with broad place and moat, but in troublous times."

In Nehemiah's prophetic book [16] we read that a command of this type was given: "...in the month of Nisan (March/April), in the twentieth year of Artaxerxes the king." This was the great Persian leader, Artaxerxes Longimatus (son of Xerxes) who ruled the Archamedenid Empire from 465 to 424 BC. [17] From the above prophecy, subtracting the seven weeks, or years, as we have seen them to be, Daniel the Hebrew predicted the 483 years from the going forth to rebuild Jerusalem, the Messiah would be revealed in Israel. Some have considered this to be the predicted time. I doubted it. The result of this will be covered in the last chapter of this book, when I reveal my conclusion. After much digging, this was to be a main key to establishing my theory.

This was also prophesied in the Tanakh, [18] as were his betrayal, [19] the price of it, [20] his piercing, his beating, and being spit upon; [21] his treatment as a criminal, or 'transgressor,' [22] his rejection by his people, [23] his refusal to defend himself, [24] his suffering crucifixion and 'casting lots' for his robe. [25] Even his riding into Jerusalem on a donkey (the colt of an ass) was predicted. [26] Many other prophecies are also uncannily fulfilled in the person of Jesus of Nazareth.

The odds are one in 84 x 10 to the 123rd power of these minute prophecies being fulfilled in one person, humanly viewed. [27]

Chapter Three

The Coming Kingdom: Prophecies Divided

Since so many prophecies point to Jesus as the Anointed One of Israel, why did he not fulfill his entire mission when living on earth 2,000 years ago? Israel was much in need of a leader to deliver them from Roman oppression. What happened? Did the plan of Jesus fail?

From his words to his disciples near the end, it is clear that Jesus was keenly aware of his immediate fate. He was also aware of the bigger picture.

The Old Testament scriptures concerning the Messiah had predictions of both the time of Jesus' earthly life and ministry, and his second advent. The Jewish Rabbis failed to see this, because there was no division given in the Nivi'im or the Kethuvim, which also contained prophetic passages, particularly in Psalms and Daniel.

The prophecies in Psalm 2 refer to both fulfilled predictions and those yet to take place.

"Why are the nations in an uproar? And why do the peoples mutter in vain?

"The kings of the earth stand up, and the rulers take counsel together, against the Lord, and against His anointed: Let us break their hands asunder, and cast away their cords from us.

"He that sitteth in heaven laugheth, the Lord hath them in derision.

"Then will He speak unto them in His wrath, and affright them in His sore displeasure: Truly it is I that have established My king upon Zion, My holy mountain.

"I will tell of the decree: the Lord said unto me: Thou art my son, this day have I begotten thee.

"Ask of Me, and I will give the nations for thy inheritance, and the ends of the earth for thy possession.

"Thou shall break them with a rod of iron; thou shalt dash them in pieces like a potter's vessel." (The Tanakh [1])

Opponents of Christianity have assigned this to Solomon and other kings. This does not hold water. The King James translation of *mashi'ahh* uses Anointed One in verse two, as it is clearly indicating one future leader. Anointed One is the correct interpretation of the word Messiah. The begetting of the Messiah, son (*beni*) of God, had already taken place (verse seven), but verses eight and nine are futuristic. All of the nations of the earth will someday be given to the Messiah for His inheritance. This is a royal Coronation Psalm. One day it will be fully fulfilled. But when? Why not already?

Numbers, the third book of the law, even contains a prophetic reference not yet fulfilled:

"I see him, but not now; I behold him, but not on high; there shall step forth a star out of Jacob, and a scepter shall rise out of Israel, and shall smite through the corners of Moab, and break down all the sons of Seth." [2]

But why two appearances of the Messiah? The Apostle Paul, in his first epistle to the Corinthians, says:

"But the natural man receiveth not **the things of the Spirit of God** for they are foolishness unto him: neither can he know them, because they are spiritually discerned." [3]

The first advent of Christ was to prepare a people for his final coming, as the Lion of the Tribe of Judah. [4]

Jesus saw the bigger picture, though his human side wished for a way of escape. [5] And though they did not understand at his death, it is quite evident that the mixed band of followers who had deserted him at his arrest believed so strongly in his resurrection and coming kingship that they kept their faith to the death of martyrdom. [6] They believed that he was indeed, not only the Messiah, but the divine son of YHWH. Contrary to those who claim that this creed was originated by the Apostle Paul, it is certain that the writers of the canonic gospels proclaimed him thus. [7][8][9] (John, Thomas in the gospel attributed to John, a quotation from Jesus himself in the Gospel of John) [10] (Matthew, quoting Jesus), as well as the writer of Hebrews. [11][12]

Still, the most miraculous testimony to the validity of the Scripture is the remarkable fulfillment of prophecy.

Chapter Four

End-time Prophecies of Jesus

At the conclusion of chapter one, I promised to later analyze Jesus' predictions of the end of the age, which he shared with his disciples.

When asked the sign of his coming as the Christ in his kingdom, and the end of the *aión*, or age, Jesus answered:

"Take heed that no man deceive you. For many shall come in my name, saying I am Christ; and shall deceive many." (**Sign number one, false messiahs**)

"And you shall hear of wars and rumors of wars; see that ye be not troubled; *for all these things* must come to pass, but the end is not yet. For nation shall rise up against nation, and kingdom against kingdom; (**Sign number two; numerous widespread wars**)

and there shall be famines and pestilences, and earthquakes in divers places. (**Sign number three, extreme natural disasters**)

"All these are the beginning of sorrows. Then they shall deliver you up to be afflicted, and shall kill you; and you shall be hated of all nations for my name's sake. (**Sign number four, persecution and hatred of followers of Jesus**)

"And then shall many be offended, and shall betray one another. And many false prophets shall deceive many. And because iniquity shall abound, the love of many shall wax cold. (**Sign number five, after slander of Christians, false prophets would move in and deceive multitudes; love of many shall wax cold**)

"But he that endures to the end, the same shall be saved **(Sign number six, persecution brings out the true followers of Christ which will eventually be rewarded for their faithfulness)**

"And this gospel of the kingdom shall be preached in all the world (Greek *oikoumene'*, the inhabited world) for a witness to all nations, and then shall the end come. **(Sign number seven, the 'Good News' of the true Christ preached around the world)**

"When therefore you see the abomination of desolation spoken of by Daniel the prophet, stand in the holy place, (whoso readeth, let him understand;) then let him which be in Judea flee into the mountains; let him which is on the housetop not come down to take any thing out of his house; neither let him which is in the field return back to take his clothes. **(Sign number eight, abomination of desolation)** [1] "And woe to them that are with child in those days!

"But pray that your flight be not in the winter, neither on the Sabbath day; For then shall be great tribulation, such as was not since the beginning of the world to this time, no, nor ever shall be. And except those days be shortened, there should **no flesh be saved**; but for the elect's sake those days shall be shortened. **(Sign number nine, unprecedented worldwide death and destruction; the tribulation begins)**

"Then if any man say *unto* you, Lo, here *is* Christ, or there, believe *it* not. For there shall arise false Christs and false prophets, and shall show signs and wonders, insomuch that if it were possible, they shall deceive the very elect. **(Sign number ten, worldwide delusion, distortion of biblical truths)**

"Behold, I have told you before. Wherefore if they say unto you, Behold, he is in the desert, go not forth; behold *he is* in the secret chamber; believe *it* not.

"For as the lightening cometh forth out of the east, and shineth even unto the west, so shall also the coming of the Son of man be.

"For wheresoever the carcass is, there will the eagles be gathered together,

"<u>Immediately after the tribulation of those days</u> shall the sun be darkened and the moon not give her light, and the stars shall fall from heaves, and the powers of the heavens shall be shaken **(Sign number eleven, solar eclipse followed by a meteor shower)**

"And **then** shall appear the sign of the Son of man in heaven; and then shall all the tribes of the earth morn, and **then shall they see the Son of man coming** in the clouds of heaven with power and great glory. **(Sign number twelve, his coming is AFTER the tribulation and the heavenly signs)**

"And he shall send his angels with a great sound of a trumpet, and they shall gather together his elect from one end of heaven to the other." [2] **(Note: the gathering of the elect is NOT UNTIL the second coming)**

Chapter Five

Sign Number One: False Messiahs

Remember that a messiah to the Jewish peoples was to be a king anointed by YHWH to save Israel from their bondage and establish them as an independent nation, as Saul, who was first called God's anointed, once did, but who, due to his turn from godliness, lost the dynasty before it began, to a shepherd boy named David. With him, God established his royal lineage for all ages.

The Israelites were looking for an earthly king, nothing more. As I stated earlier, they did not comprehend the big picture. The Creator is quoted by the prophet Isaiah as saying, "For my thoughts are not your thoughts, neither are your ways my ways." [1] God is ahead of our thought patterns because he is God. He is the source of all life, and the prototype by which good and evil are determined. We see in the temporal world of finite man; he sees in the eternal world of infinite God.

False messiahs began immediately after the time of Jesus' earthly ministry. The first such 'messiah' was Simon Bar Kobba, in the second century after Jesus. He was the leader of the Jewish military rebellion in 132 AD in Palestine. According to Wayne Simpson of the Biblical Research Foundation (in part):

"The Emperor Hadrian announced that he would turn Jerusalem into a Roman colony. Rebellion promptly broke out. While Rabbi Akiba was recognized as a spiritual Leader of that time, he was not a military man and could not lead the Jews into their ultimate battle. Into this leadership void stepped a Charismatic leader, Simon Bar Kokhba [note: born Simon ben Koseva], who suddenly burst on the scene, rallying support for rebellion. Akiba was quick to proclaim Bar Kokhba 'a messianic king!' He applied a Bible verse directly to him 'a star, kokhab, has arisen out of Jacob' (ref: Numbers 24:17). So Simon became known as Bar Kohba, Son of the

Star. His mission became clear and sanctioned by rabbinical authority. For a people starved for hope, the approval of Akiba was more than enough proof of Bar Kokhba's authenticity. Curiously, it was in the Roman writings of the time, rather than the Jewish writings, that miraculous powers were attributed to him.

"He was said to have been able to call forth fire at his command.

"His goals were clearly the freedom of his people, the glory of Judaism, and the liberation of his homeland.

"With his great charisma and leadership, he attracted Jewish warriors from all over the world to fight in his epic final battle against the mighty Roman Empire.

"When Bar Kokhba's forces recaptured Jerusalem, there was wild speculation that the Temple, which had been laid in ruins for sixty two years, might be rebuilt by this new Messiah. But this was not to be because of the preoccupation of carrying on the war. Interestingly, Jewish sovereignty did allow for the minting of coins that appeared with Bar Kokhba's likeness bearing a pot of manna and the rod of Aaron, unmistakable symbols of the Messiah.

"In relatively short order, over 50 forts, 985 cities, and all of Judea, Samaria, and Galilee fell to Bar Kokhba.

"While the consequences of this uprising were finally realized by the Emperor, he placed the military operations in the hands of Julius Serverus, the most successful Roman commander.

"Serverus understood that fighting an essentially guerilla army in the classic tradition would be problematic. His strategy was to surround and besiege the rebels in their strongholds, forcing them into starvation. By this tactic, one-by-one, the Jewish citadels fell.

"After about an entire year under the onslaught of the mighty Roman army, Betar fell and close to half a million Jews were massacred.

"This defeat was so devastating to Jewish messianic hopes that anticipation of the future redemption was ended for centuries." [2]

Next came Moses of Crete, in the fifth century, then no other until David Altoy in the twelfth century began a string of hopeful messiahs which would arise a minimum of one per century: Abraham Ben Samuel Abulafa (1240-1291), David Reuveni (1400-1538), Issac Luria (1534-1574), Hayyim Vital (1542-1620), Shabbatai Zevi (1826-1676), Jacob Frank (1726-1791), and finally, in our generation, would come Rebbe Menechem Mendel Schneerson (1902-1994).

Simpson tells us:

"Four color literature was distributed explaining that Schneerson was the subject of the age old Jewish longing:

"'Yes, we are talking about the King Messiah who will redeem us in the near future. Indeed, the Jewish leader, religious foundation of the world from the Davidic dynasty, who works to extend the influence of Torah and mitzvot to all of Israel, who in the future will build the third temple and gather in the exiles. This is the same person who also prepared the nations of the world for a life of righteousness, and who will unite humanity around belief in one God. It is the Lubavitcher Rebbe...the King Messiah.

"At that time the fervor of Messiah Schneerson reached its peak. Rumors spread that he was to be crowned 'King Messiah' on January 31, 1993. A large crowd of jubilant supporters gathered outside Chabad headquarters in Crown Heights [Brooklyn, NY] to see if Schneerson would accept the messianic mantle. But just before the Rebbe appeared to the crowd, one of the aids announced that his appearance should not be interpreted as having anything to do with a coronation.

"It was clear that, once again, he wanted to distance himself from any claim that he was the messiah. As soon as he appeared, his followers began singing 'Long live our master, rebbe, and teacher, King Messiah'. Louder and louder they sang as they repeated this refrain. The rebbe did not, indeed could not speak. He merely nodded his head in time to the music. After a few minutes the curtain around, the rebbe's balcony was drawn and he did not re-appear. After a couple of hours, the crowd began to disperse.

"But a few months later, the Rebbe was dead. The Lubavitcher community fell silent in shock and disbelief. Their leader had fallen and there was no immediate successor. In disarray, they grieved their loss. Most accepted the reality that he could not be the messiah that they had longed for.

"As it often happens in the face of such resolute eschatological expectations, some die hard followers have voiced their expectations that their Rebbe will be raised from the dead. Rather than accept the sudden disappointment, they continue to have blind faith that Schneerson is the messiah.

"How many others will there be? It will only end when the messiah finally comes." [3]

From this, it is obvious that Jesus' prediction of false messiahs has been fulfilled.

Chapter Six

Sign Number Two: Wars and Rumors of Wars

The prediction of 'wars and rumors of wars' may seem like an easily foretold prophecy to those critics of the Christ. War is a constant factor in the ever-changing landscape and rulership of the world.

But the prophecies of Jesus are fitting into a time period, or sequences of events, when war would be overwhelming, and Israel would be at the focus of the conflicts. Until 1948, for many centuries, there was no nation known as Israel. There are those who see this as other nations which fulfill the prophecies of Israel, comprised by members of the 'lost tribes.' The conquest of Europe by William of Normandy and the subsequent spread of Christianity are certainly factors in the alignment of the nations in such a way that the prophecies of Jesus are happening today before our eyes; also the spread of Islam and the never-ending battles over the land we now know as Israel, has placed the Middle East at the center of world strife in our day.

Before 9-11 (2001), no one would have dreamed of terrorists striking the United States by high-jacking planes and flying them into the twin towers at the World Trade Center in Manhattan. I initially wrote these words in 2007, and yet, even into today, the conflict rages on in the Middle East with America and an enemy difficult to define—terrorism based on radical extremism, rather than merely Islam versus Judaism, or the descendants of Ishmael and Abraham's other sons, versus those of Isaac. These radicals view the U.S. in the same light as Israel; they see us as Zionists, as their allies, and because of this, an enemy to their cause.

This alignment is the situation to which Jesus was referring in Matthew 24:6.

Before there was a nation called Israel, during the days of captivity and dispersion, the prophecies could not take place. Only beginning in 1948, with the acceptance of Israel by major world powers, could these predictions begin to unveil in a definite pattern. The twentieth century has been portrayed as *'The Century of Warfare'* in a 26-part British TV documentary by that title released in 1993. [1] Just prior to Israel's becoming a nation, a primary focus in World War II was the Holocaust; Nazi extermination of millions of Jews in unimaginable death camps, and the harsh denial of civil rights, not only of Jews, but anyone sympathetic to their cause. From the ashes of their deep shame came the victory of independence.

In Jesus' day, he looked down through time and predicted the rising conflicts of our day. "Nation will rise against nation, and kingdom against kingdom." This is a clear picture of the world in which we live. More than ever, this appears to be fact, and with our modern media, we are too keenly aware of the atrocities of war around the globe. In the twenty-first century, like never before, Israel is at the heart of world conflict.

Chapter Seven

Sign Number Three: Extreme Natural Disasters

From the great deluge to the "fire from heaven" which destroyed Sodom and Gomorrah, to the plagues of Egypt which brought to fruition the exodus from Egypt, the Israelites were familiar with the disaster legends of their history.

Though volcanoes were not mentioned, they have caused many famines and much loss of life. The ancient world would not wait long to see the replay of the story of Sodom and Gomorrah, for only nine years after Christ's prediction of the destruction of the Temple in Jerusalem was fulfilled, the eruption of Vesuvius in 79 AD brought about the tragic and sudden culmination of the thriving Roman city of Pompeii, covering it in ash, and preserving it in rock, to be all but forgotten until its excavation in 1748.

Between 1600 and 1983, Indonesia, (which was struck in December 2004 by the horrible tsunami, and less disastrous ones in 2010 and 2018) suffered over 160,000 deaths from volcano eruptions, many of which were caused by starvation.

Volcanoes are a major harbinger of famine, one of the signs mentioned by Jesus at this time. Famine, properly defined, is a phenomenon in which a large percentage of the population of a region or country becomes so undernourished that death by starvation becomes increasingly common. [1] Famine in Africa, particularly in Sudan, Niger and Ethiopia have claimed countless lives.

In the last two centuries, there have been two prior major famines: The Great Irish Potato Famine, known in Gaelic as 'Au Gorta Mor' [2] (1846-1850), and The Great Famine of the Soviet Ukraine, which claimed multiplied thousands of peasants' lives between 1921 and 1933, leaving their bony remains strewn askew on boards and earth. [3]

Recent times have been unprecedented in all of history for the vast volume of nature's wrath.

The year 2004 witnessed some of the worst and deadliest disasters of nature in decades, including earthquakes, typhoons and hurricanes. So overwhelming were the losses, that the United Nations felt compelled to hold a disaster reduction conference in Kobe, Japan, the day after the tenth anniversary of the great Hanshin earthquake. [4] On the heels of a harsh year of loss of lives in other phenomena, on December 26, the magnitude 9.9 earthquake in the Indian Ocean triggered the fierce tsunami, which I mentioned earlier, taking more than 200,000 lives in twelve countries, again hitting Indonesia hardest. [5] Even newscasters were calling it a disaster of 'Biblical proportions.'

When it seemed that we could stand no more, 2005 brought another rash of nature's wrath. China alone stated that 2,475 lives were lost there, due to natural disasters, including typhoons and floods. [6]

In the U.S., it was the worst year on record for hurricanes, running the full alphabet, and carrying into Greek letters for names. The most costly and damaging of these being Katrina, which, as a category five storm, swept across the Gulf states of Louisiana, Mississippi and Alabama, virtually paralyzing New Orleans, causing many to feel that the city would never recover.

Thousands of evacuees relocated, in other states, and will never return; according to 2007 reports, as many as 80%. [7] A large percentage of the damage was done when the levees burst, separating Lake Pontchartrain from the city. Flooding about 80% of it, [8] and laying the upper ninth ward in utter devastation. Katrina was responsible for $75 billion in damage, making it the costliest hurricane in history. At least 1,383 deaths are blamed on this incredibly devastating storm. Other areas affected include South Florida, the Bahamas, and Cuba.

According to Dr. Mark Jacobson, associate professor of civil and environmental engineering at Stanford University in California, the higher temperatures of the ocean and atmosphere caused by global warming have likely been causing hurricanes since the late twentieth century to gain in intensity and possibly in frequency as well. [9] This is also causing a rise in the oceans and may be responsible for the unheard-of snowfall which occurred in southern California in February and March, 2006. An article by Chris Dolce and Jonathan Belles published on weather.com on January 25, 2017 was titled *Januburied: Snow Breaks Record in Sierra Nevada*, in which it is stated that that month alone more than 20 feet of snow had fallen in parts of the Sierra Nevada, and that Mammoth Mountain had set a new all-time snowfall record.

Famines predicted by African scientists at the date of my original manuscript have come to pass with alarming accuracy. An article in *The Economist* (March 30, 2017) was titled *Famine Menaces 20 m People in Africa and Yeman.* [10] The article is subtitled 'The Return of the Third Horseman,' having an unmistakable reference to the biblical Apocalypse. Though caused more by war than drought, the result is the same.

On October 8, 2005, an earthquake measuring 7.6 on the Richter scale rocked northern Pakistan, near Islamabad, leaving thousands dead, and multitudes more homeless, not only in Pakistan, but also in India and Afghanistan. [11] Almost 20,000 lost their lives within the first day and 41,000 more were injured. [12]

In early 2006, nature's trend continued; Indonesia being devastated, once again, by the loss of thousands more lives in a magnanimous 6.3 earthquake in the early morning hours of Saturday, May 27. While the hurricane season brought fewer disasters than the two previous years because of the El Niño effect, early 2007 saw freaky weather patterns around the world, and overall the warmest winter on record.

A pestilence is an epidemic (in some cases even a pandemic) of a virulent and highly contagious disease. [13] Cholera and bubonic plague are examples of this. Bird flu, which was a huge concern a few years back, and especially the deadly H5N1 strain which continues to spread in poultry in Egypt and certain parts of Asia, could become a severe example of this. [14]

These signs which Jesus said would come to pass near the end of the age are echoed in the four horsemen of the Apocalypse in the Book of the Revelation of Jesus Christ written by St. John the Evangelist, traditionally identified as the Apostle John, during his exile on the Isle of Patmos in the Aegean Sea off the coast of Greece. The vision of John coincides with prophecies of both Daniel and Jesus.

Chapter Eight

Sign Number Four: Persecution and Hatred of Followers of Jesus

In some parts of the world, followers of Jesus have always been hated. Persecution of the disciples and early church leaders led to their martyrdom. The Crusades pitted Christians against Islamic invaders and sought to protect pilgrims on their journeys to the Holy Land. Missionaries have often been the target of hatred and murder, especially in Communist countries.

But to truly understand where we are in the flow of "end-time" events prophesied by Jesus the Christ, we must look hard at this prediction. Some relate this to Israel. But Jesus stated plainly that their opponents would kill them for **HIS** name's sake. The nation of Israel has not accepted Jesus as the Messiah. This is clearly referring to followers of Jesus as the Christ. Since the extreme natural disasters are clearly happening in the twenty-first century more than ever, and these prophecies follow a progression of one after the other, it is impossible not to assert the fact that this is yet to be fulfilled; but as we shall soon see, it is to happen quickly. Signs five and six have already begun to manifest themselves and are hastily becoming discernible on the horizon, even more visibly today than the date of the original manuscript of this book.

There is a growing attack on Christianity today by secular education, gays, Muslims and other groups. *Life Magazine*, MSNBC and politicians have noticed.

Chapter Nine

Sign Number Five: False Prophets Deceive Many, Love Will Grow Cold

In the past century, strange new religions have taken root worldwide. There have been numerous groups which have proclaimed themselves as the only true church. Cults have taken their adherents down the road to destruction and suicide in the presumed authority of God. The names of David Koresh and Jim Jones have been placed in the cult hall of fame, so to speak.

Koresh was born Vernon Wayne Howell in Houston, Texas in 1959, to a single mother. He was reared by his maternal grandparents, and never knew his father. Being lonely; also dyslexic, he dropped out of high school. He was, however, interested in music and the Bible. By age 12, he had memorized large portions of the scripture, and by age 20, he became a Seventh Day Adventist, his mother's faith. But even there he did not fit in, and was expelled for his 'bad influence' on the youth. He moved to Hollywood in an effort to become a rock star, failing once again. In 1981, he joined the Branch Davidians, a sect which had settled near Waco, Texas in 1935. Before long, he had an affair with their prophetess, Lois Roden, then in her late sixties, traveling with her to Israel. After her death, he struggled with her son, George, for control of the sect.

For a time, Koresh and his believers moved away, but upon their return, a gunfight ensued in which Roden was injured. On trial for attempted murder, Koresh was acquitted, and by 1990 he had become the leader of the Branch Davidians, legally changing his name, stating his belief that he was now the leader of the biblical House of David (Koresh being Hebrew for Cyrus, the Persian king who released the Jews held in Babylonian captivity to return to their homeland). [1]

The rest of the story is well known. A raid in February 1993, by the Bureau of Alcohol, Tobacco and Firearms, led to the 51 day siege by the FBI and the standoff, ending in April, when the sect's ranch, known as Mount Carmel, was burned, supposedly by the Davidians. The inhabitants, including Koresh, who had been wounded earlier, and later shot in the head, were all found dead. Based on prophecies of Daniel, [2] the Branch Davidians believed that Koresh would one day return to earth. The most common date for this was 1,335 days from his death; December 14, 1996 [3] (December 14 was the birth date of Japanese Emperor Go-Suzaku, *1009;* French astronomer and physic, Nostradamus, *1503* and King George VI of the United Kingdom, *1895*).

An earlier example of a strange cult leader was Jim Jones, who was born in Indiana in 1931. After leaving his position as minister with mainstream protestant denomination, "Disciples of Christ," he became the head of People's Temple (originally Wings of Deliverance), and became a champion of racial equality and social justice. Jones wrote a book in which he stated that the Bible contained many contradictions, but also contained truths. He declared himself to be an incarnation of Jesus, Akenaten, Buddha, Lenin and Father Divine (an earlier self-styled, want-to-be deity). He claimed to perform miracles of healing to attract new followers, who called him 'Dad.'

In 1977, most of the 1,000 members of his church moved from San Francisco to Guyana, after an investigation for tax evasion began. Jones named his settlement Jonestown. He attempted to build a utopian society free from racism based on quasi-communistic principles. Followers who refused to go to Guyana told stories of brutal beatings, murders, and a mass suicide plan, but were not believed. There were also reports that Jones was addicted to drugs. Of the group who accompanied Jones, about 70% were black and impoverished.

In November 1978, Congressman Leo Ryan led a fact-finding mission to Jonestown, following the above allegations. They spent three days interviewing residents, but left suddenly after an attempt was made on the life of the congressman. They took with them twenty church members who wished to leave, and were fired upon at the airstrip. Five people were killed, including two NBC employees. Later that same day, November 18, 1973, the remaining 914 residents of Jonestown, 276 of which were children, committed mass suicide upon Jones' instructions, by either drinking Flavor Aid laced with cyanide, forced cyanide injections, or shooting. Jones himself was found dead, shot in the head, much like his counterpart, Koresh. [4]

The latest in this string was Puerto Rican born Jose Luis De Jesus Miranda (1946-2013), who was the leader of the Creciendo en Gracia cult, headquartered in Miami, Florida. With millions of followers around the world, he claimed to be both the returned Jesus Christ and the Antichrist, was famous for making statements opposing the Roman Catholic Church, and had a personal interpretation of the Bible. He reportedly believed that there is no devil and that prayer does no good. Before taking this name, he used the moniker *Jesucristo Hombre* (The Man Jesus Christ). Shortly after his death, his followers granted him the title of Melchizedek, (taken from the mysterious personage in the Old Testament to which Abraham first paid tithes) meaning Justice and King of Peace. [5]

Though false prophets and would-be messiahs have arrived, this does not constitute the entire completion of the predictions of Jesus in this passage. The next part states, "the love of many will wax cold." It is certain that this is also happening, but not yet to the degree that it will in the end. It has been said that if the present trend continues, within the next generation we could be living in a godless society.

Dr. Creflo Dollar, a fiery minister, and founder of the World Changer's Ministry in Atlanta (a global Christian organization headquartered at his 30,000 member church, World Changers International), authored an editorial on this very subject, expressing his grave concerns.

He stated that the writers of the First Amendment did not intend that freedom of religion mean freedom from religion, a statement which has been adopted by other Evangelicals since then. He said that the First Amendment was meant to prevent establishment of a national church, such as happened in England. Dollar quoted the following statement from Thomas Jefferson:

"I contemplate with solemn reverence that act of the whole American people which declared that their legislature should 'make no law respecting an establishment of religion, or **prohibiting the free exercise thereof**,' thus building a wall of separation of church and State."

He further cited his disdain over the ruling of California that it was unconstitutional to recite the Pledge of Allegiance in schools because it contains the words, "one nation under God." [6]

Many Christian groups had expressed their concerns many years ago over actions by atheist Madelyn Murray O'Hair which resulted in the removal of Bible reading from public schools in the U.S. in 1963. In Houston, Texas, for example, an organization has been formed known as Huston Atheist Society, promoting the rights of persons to have no religion, and supporting political candidates which agree with their views. [7] But humanism is far from new and secularist societies exist around the world.

Since God is the embodiment of love, when He is removed from our public life, and our next generation is encouraged to rebel against religious authorizes, it is only natural that this would result in a society which is not concerned with a moral code of ethics. This is evident today in all facets of business and government.

But in the very end, society will become more godless than even we could possibly imagine.

Chapter Ten

Sign Number Six: Persecution Separates the Believers from Unbelievers

People who have lived in third-world countries will testify to the fact that in these areas, there is no division of the "Body of Christ." All who have a Christian faith meet together and share their faith. There is no concern as to whether one is a Baptist, a Methodist, a Presbyterian, a Catholic or a Charismatic. America, with churches 'on every corner,' has grown 'gospel hardened.' Our entertainment media both here, in Canada and the United Kingdom have gone so far from faith and family values which have been our trademark for generations, that we are sliding 'down the rabbit hole' at an alarming rate.

When the prophecies of the very end are finally fulfilled, there will come a solid uniting of believers in the Lordship and divinity of Jesus as the Christ. Persecution has a way of strengthening faith. When this comes, no one will have to tell Christians that this prophecy has been fulfilled: all will know. When the early church began being persecuted, there was a bonding together. During World War II, the Allied Nations felt a kinship, all fighting together for a victory over a common known enemy: Nazism. The bonding of the final church will be on that order; a bonding that is yet to happen.

Chapter Eleven

Sign Number Seven: The Gospel of the Kingdom Will be Preached in All the World

Preachers who claim that all prophecies before the coming of the Lord have been fulfilled fail to see the clear picture. They are expecting a 'rapture' or in the biblical terms, 'catching away,' to occur before the Second Coming. I will cover this, in more detail, later.

In the twelve years since the original manuscript of this text was written in 2007; to date, this prophecy has not yet come to pass. However, great strides have been made toward this end by the tearing down of the 'iron curtain' in the summer of 1989 [1] and the Berlin Wall dividing East and West Germany in November of that year, [2] signifying the end of the former Soviet Union. The establishment of the initial trade agreement between the U.S. and China by President Richard Nixon in 1972 has also helped. These factors have given access to the respective countries for Christianity in a way not possible prior to these events.

When I was in Beijing in June, 2006, I spent a lot of time in one of the largest bookstores in all of China. There are many floors containing books in numerous languages, including English. One surprising fact was that there were plenty of Bibles available for sale there. The acceptance of Christianity in some parts of the former Soviet Union has also made it more acceptable in these countries than in "Christian America." Australia, with only about seven percent of its peoples claiming any religious faith, has no restrictions on teaching Christianity in their schools, according to a family friend of mine who is currently teaching there.

Wycliffe Bible Translators have long recognized the need to translate the Bible into every dialect on the planet; as a result, they have been working on that goal for a number of years.

As of October, 2017, the entire Bible had been translated into 670 languages. The New Testament has been translated into 1,521 languages and portions of the Bible into 1,121 other dialects.

Wycliffe's ongoing project to accomplish this massive goal is called *Vision 2025*. Their most optimistic target date to reach the entire world with Scripture is the year 2025. According to their current statement, "But unless people have the Bible in the language they understand best, they cannot read this message of life, hope and salvation. Millions of people don't have a single verse of Scripture." [3]

Implications of the necessity of this goal becoming a reality will be more readily understandable by reading the remaining chapters of this book.

If the Christians could be 'raptured' at any moment, this scripture would never be fulfilled.

Chapter Twelve

Sign Number Eight: The Abomination of Desolation

Jesus said, "When therefore you see the abomination of desolation spoken of by Daniel the prophet, stand in the holy place, (whoso readeth, let him understand:) then let him which be in Judea flee into the mountains; let him which is on the housetop not come down to take any thing out of the house; neither let him which is in the field return back to take his clothes." [1]

The visible presence of the 'abomination of desolation' was to be the final sign that the second phase of the 'Great Tribulation' had begun. To understand what this is, we must turn to the passage to which Jesus is referring, Daniel 9:27:

"And he shall confirm the covenant with many for one week: and in the midst of the week he shall cause the sacrifice and the oblation to cease, and for the overspreading of the abominations he shall make *it* desolate, even until the consummation, and that determined shall be poured upon the desolate."

This week is known to most students of Bible prophecy as "Daniel's seventieth week." Here is the evident division in the weeks of Daniel. The final week predicted here has never come to pass. This confusing week is the key to these prophecies. But why? And what Covenant? Who is involved? What is the week?

The Hebrew words originally used in Daniel for abomination of desolation are הַשִּׁקֻּץ מְשׁוֹמֵם (*ha-shikkuts meshomem*), Baal of heaven, a title found in Phoenician and Aramaic inscriptions, and the Semitic equivalent of the Greek, *Zeus*, Jupiter. Here it is modified by the prophet Daniel through Jewish aversion for the name of a pagan god. [2]

Bible scholars, through the years, have identified this as various desecrations of the Temple at Jerusalem, including its occupation by the Zealots, the destruction of it by Titus in 70 AD, and the building of the wooden mosque before the Dome of the Rock (*Qubbat as-Sakhrah* in Arabic) was constructed as a shrine for pilgrims between 685 and 691. One thing upon which all seem to agree is that the Temple is desecrated by setting up worship of a pagan god there. There was even a declaration in 1997 that a Peace Agreement entered into by Rabin with Palestinians constituted this abomination, thrusting us into the Great Tribulation. If this had been true, we would be completely through the Great Tribulation by now.

The Hebrew word used for week, *shabowa*, indicated seven; in this case, most Fundamentalist Bible scholars agree that it means a period of seven years. According to the progression which we have seen with the fulfillment of prophecy, it is obvious that we have certainly not entered into this "week of years," but with the most recent events, we could be alarmingly close.

The nation of Israel has been making plans to rebuild the Temple for many years. The problem has been that the Temple Mount is a place so holy to both Jews and Arabs that they refuse to share it. A great deal of speculation has arisen about what treasures may have been recovered during the Crusades when the Knights Templar were headquartered there during the twelfth and thirteenth centuries, and what may have happened to them after the Templars were rounded up and executed in 1307.

This subject is a primary quest being examined on the current History Channel series, *The Curse of Oak Island*, another premise with which I have been personally aware and involved, long before the series began. In fact, I was originally slated to publish *The Templar Mission to Oak Island and Beyond: Search for Ancient Secrets: the Shocking Revelations of a 12th Century Manuscript* by the late Zena Halpern, used on the show by Rick and Marty Lagina.

Zena and I spent much time working on publication plans before another friend of mine agreed to help; he completed the necessary edits so that she could self-publish in 2017.

In the past 150 years, a number of archeological excavations have been made under the Temple Mount. They were first undertaken by British Royal Engineers in the 1870s. After the Six-Day War in June 1967, in which divine aid was claimed, Israel took control of the Old City. Excavations have been conducted since then, by Israel and the Jerusalem Islamic Waqf, the Muslim authority in charge of the Al-Aqsa Mosque, which have been criticized. Right after the war, the Ministry of Religious Affairs began the excavations intended to expose the continuation of the Western Wall.

These excavations, lasting almost twenty years, have revealed many previously unknown facts about the history and geography of the Temple Mound. In 1996, Israeli Prime Minister Benjamin Netanyahu opened the Western Wall Tunnel near the site. My pastor, Rev. Dr. Jacqueline De Berry, was privileged to explore this amazing Western Wall Tunnel in 2007.

The nation of Israel is in constant turmoil; the Palestinian Islam Arabs have a deep desire to bring termination to the state of Israel, thereby returning to a solely Palestinian state.

Jerusalem is the holy city of all streams of Abrahamic faith, including Christianity. Control of Jerusalem is the blockade of peace in Israel. On December 6, 2017, U.S. President Donald Trump announced the United States recognition of Jerusalem as the capital of Israel, and ordered the relocation of the U.S. Embassy from Tel Aviv to Jerusalem. His decision, however, was rejected by the majority of world leaders. [3] Although the United Nations Security Council condemned Trump's decision, some countries supported the move, and the Embassy was relocated. Christian leaders were divided on this, but Texas mega church pastor and televangelist John Hagee, [4] now internationally famous for his controversial best-selling 2013 prophetic book *Four Blood Moons*, was in the U.S. delegation at the Embassy's dedication on May 14, 2018.

In the book, Hagee revisits the history of blood moons, including the one which occurred at the miraculous Six Day War in Israel in 1967, and looks at four such moons beginning in 2014, culminating with the mystically rare 'Super Wolf Blood Moon' which appeared over Washington, DC (and all of the Western Hemisphere) at midnight, January 20, 2019, quoting Bible prophecies which he feels coincide with this. Several other Evangelical ministers have now jumped on board the bandwagon, stating that this latter event, accompanied by other phenomena, is a harbinger of the impending end of the age.

Many believe that World War III will be fought over occupation of the Temple Mount. Some have expressed concerns about America's relationship with Israel, and feel that by continuing the 'war on terror' started by George W. Bush, our government is taking on the entire Islamic world. America, however, in the past, has given many millions of dollars to the Palestinians under Hamas, [5] which runs the Gaza Strip, and whose regime is still set on annihilation of Israel.

Hezbollah, meaning 'Party of God,' [6] is an Iranian-Syrian backed Shiite political party formed in 1982 for the purpose of combating Israeli forces occupying Southern Lebanon. Its primary wing is the Jihad Council, and its political wing is Loyalty to the Resistance Block party in the Lebanese parliament. Since the invasion of Lebanon in 1982, in support of the Free Lebanese State, Israel has occupied a strip in Southern Lebanon.

Heavy attacks and bombings in ongoing military strikes on Beirut and Southern Lebanon in 2006 lasted over a month, until a fragile cease fire was reached by the U.N. in August. A national unity government was formed in 2008.

ISIS, aka ISIL, has caused continued U.S. occupation of Afghanistan during the Obama and early Trump years, as well as Syria, which Trump has vowed to discontinue.

In truth, the Temple must be rebuilt before this prophecy can be fulfilled. Before this happens, the conflict must end; but, again, recent events have occurred which are changing the scope of this as never before. We will get to those shortly.

The scripture will be fulfilled when the false messiah, known universally by Christians as the Anti-Christ, Greek ἀντίχριστος, meaning 'instead of Christ,' [7] stands in the Most High Place in the Third Temple and **declares himself to be the incarnation of God**. Though the term 'Anti-Christ' appears in none of the prophetic scriptures regarding the charismatic leader who will claim to be the incarnation of God, [8] he is certainly portrayed in this light. Where the term is used, by the Apostle John, [9] it is meant as a false prophet or teacher, and not necessarily this person, as it is recorded once in the plural. [10] The leader referred to as the Anti-Christ, who is to appear in the end of the age, is mentioned in Paul's second epistle to the church at Thessalonica as the 'man of sin,' or 'son of perdition,' [11] and is also commonly identified with the Dragon, the Beast and False Prophet in the book of Revelation. [12]

In the passage from Thessalonians, we see the obvious application of the reference to the event of which Jesus spoke, and its tie to the Daniel prophecy:

"Let no man deceive you by any means: for *that day shall not come,* except there be a falling away first, and that man of sin be revealed, the son of perdition: who opposeth and **exalteth himself above all that is called God, or that is worshipped**, so that he sitteth in the Temple of God, **shewing himself that he is God**." [13]

The main points to remember here are: these prophecies occur <u>in succession</u>, so it has not yet transpired; to be fulfilled, the Temple must be standing in Jerusalem; the Temple has not yet been rebuilt. Very recent events, not openly being discussed in the media, may be indicating the closeness of this occurring.

On the eve of Passover, 2012, the first animal sacrifice made in Israel since biblical times was made at the foot of the Temple Mound—the required Passover lamb. White robed *Kohanim* (priests) had a handful of supporters on hand for the initial reenactment of the Passover Sacrifice. This has since been repeated for seven consecutive years, with crowds in 2018 at around 1,500. The event conforms to biblical requirements and is accompanied by music played on silver trumpets and other instruments especially made to serve in the Third Temple.

"We can see the Third Temple rising on the horizon," Shimshon Elboim, one the organizers of the event in 2018, told *Breaking Israel News*. "It used to be a small group of activists, but this year it went mainstream." [14]

These things are already visible, but this is not the shocking conclusion. I will reveal that after we look at the balance of prophecies.

Chapter Thirteen

Sign Number Nine: The Great Tribulation Begins: Worldwide Death and Destruction

It is inconceivable to think that this time has already begun. With all of the catastrophes that have been experienced in the past few years, and even as some are saying, "With all the players on the field," we haven't seen anything to compare with what is predicted for the 'Great Tribulation.'

The book of Revelation describes, in startling detail, the advent of the four horsemen of the Apocalypse, and the pouring out of the seven vials. Plagues are brought upon the earth. Many of these signs parallel the predictions of Christ for the last days. But my purpose is not to rehash each of these, but to show that strong evidence exists to suggest that nuclear war will occur at this time. The tribulation period of both Daniel and Revelation is divided into two distinct three and one-half year periods. [1] (Revelation speaks of the seven seals, seven vials, and seven trumpets), [2] reminiscent of the fat and lean years which Joseph predicted in Egypt. [3]

The first period will bring peace, making those who promoted the powerful world leader say, "We told you so!" He will be accepted as the true messiah of Israel, and his reign will be seen as the cure to all of the world's ills. He will bring about a One World Government which will surpass any utopia of the past. He will be so convincing that he would deceive even God's elect if it were possible. [4]

Daniel reveals that:

"From the time the daily sacrifice is taken away, and the abomination that maketh desolate set up, *there shall be* a thousand two hundred and ninety days." [5]

Twelve hundred and ninety days equals a three and one-half year period, or the last half of the week of years in Daniel's seventieth week; the first half being a time of peace. An earlier verse makes this clear:

"And he (Anti-Christ, son of perdition or false prince) shall confirm the covenant, for one week; and in the midst of the week he shall cause the sacrifice and oblation to cease, and for the overspreading of the abominations he shall make desolate even the consummation, and that determined shall be poured upon the desolate." [6]

The scriptures tell of a third of the angels of heaven falling with Lucifer, later equated with Satan. This story comes to mind in Revelation 8, which is replete with *one third* scenarios.

"The first angel sounded, and there followed hail and fire mingled with blood, and they were cast upon the earth; **and the third part of the trees were burned up**, and all green grass was burnt up. And the second angel sounded, and as it were a great mountain burning with fire was cast into the sea; **and the third part of the sea became blood; and the third part of the creatures which in the sea, and had life, died; and the third part of the ships were destroyed**. And the third angel sounded, and there fell a great star from heaven, burning as it were in a lamp, and it fell upon **the third part of the rivers**, and upon the fountains of the waters; And the name of the star is called Wormwood, **and the third part of the waters became wormwood**; and many died of the waters, because they were made bitter. And the fourth angel sounded, **and the third part of the sun was smitten, and the third part of the moon, and the third part of the stars; so as the third part of them were darkened; and the day shone not for the third part of it, and the night likewise**. [7]

This sounds much like the verses in Joel 2 and Acts 2 which Hagee quoted in his book and likened to the Blood Moon eclipse on January 20, 2019.

Notably, "The sun shall be turned into darkness and the moon into blood before the great and terrible day of the Lord comes." But it is certain that <u>Revelation 8 is yet to be fulfilled</u>.

Let's examine the interpretation of this passage. Something was seen as falling from the heavens like hail and blood. One third of the trees, and all of the grass of earth were burned up. One third of the sea was, or appeared to be, blood, killing one third of the life in the oceans, and destroying one third of the ships in them. A great star fell from the heavens, polluting the springs feeding one third of the rivers of earth. The star is called 'Wormwood.' It is curious that the name 'Chernobyl,' the power station in the Ukraine which experienced the nuclear disaster on March 27, 1986, is the name of a bitter herb, equal to the herb wormwood, and has the same meaning.

Whether this is coincidental or divine revelation, the devastation predicted in the visions of John on Patmos have all the implications of nuclear disaster.

The waters would become bitter, and many would die from them. The smoggy skies would block out the light of the sun in day, and the heavenly bodies by night.

On Friday, February 1, 2019, the *Washington Post* ran a story stating that President Donald Trump had announced that the U.S. was withdrawing from the nuclear arms control treaty (INF) which President Ronald Reagan signed with Russian Prime Minister Mikhail Gorbachev in 1987, stating that Russia had been violating it for years. Though denying the charge, Vladimir Putin was quick to comply. This move made it possible for both countries to overtly move forward with development and stockpiling of intermediate-range nuclear missiles, bringing the threat of nuclear war one step closer to reality.

In a nuclear war, death would wreak havoc everywhere. None would be immune from its devastating effect.

It is obvious that this is a worldwide occurrence, not just a problem for Israel, for Jesus said, "And except these days be shortened, **there should no flesh be saved**: but **for the elect's sake**, those days shall be shortened." 8 Nuclear war would certainly be such a calamity. It is called the time of Jacob's trouble, because Israel is at the heart of the problems which invoke the Great Tribulation.

Jesus makes it plain in the following verse that if someone were to tell one of his people that he has returned at this time. And he is "here or there" that they should not believe it.

Chapter Fourteen

Sign Number Ten: Delusion, Total Spiritual Perversion

When the false messiah sets up his government, he will also sanction only one religion. It will deny that Jesus was the begotten son of God, only *a messiah*, and *a son of God* in a spiritual nature, and will accept all 'prophets' as equal. He will have what he will claim is proof that Jesus was a mere man, and therefore did not rise from the dead. He will, in all likelihood claim, that he is a descendant of Jesus himself, through what was his marriage to Mary Magdalene; [1] he may possibly claim to be an incarnation of Jesus himself.

Since 1983, with the publication of the highly speculative and controversial, *Holy Blood, Holy Grail*, authored by the team of Michael Baigent, Henry Lincoln and Richard Leigh, first published in the United Kingdom, and later in America, the stage has been set for this doctrine to shift into the minds of those not rooted in Christian faith, and to "deceive the very elect if it were possible."

More than most Americans, I have been made aware of this for many years. At the end of their sequel, *The Messianic Legacy*, Baigent, Lincoln and Leigh proposed the thought to their readers that the Priory of Sion can easily produce a messiah the same kind as Jesus himself. [2]

Many books have been written about the claim of the marriage between Jesus and Mary Magdalene; indeed, many television specials have been the result. With the release, and run-away sales of Dan Brown's novel, *The Da Vinci Code* in 2003, the ball began its rapid roll; with a major motion picture in 2006, the message they wanted to convey has spread even more rapidly.

The stage is truly set for the fulfillment of this vital prophecy of the final days of our age.

As a St. Clair, I am a member of a family highly publicized in books like *Holy Blood, Holy Grail*, and *The Da Vinci Code;* as well, there are a great number of other books and films which announce this theory. Given these close connections to some of the authors, I am somewhat uniquely qualified to write on this subject. In these publications, we are said to be descendants of Jesus of Nazareth, whom it is claimed was only a man, and who fathered children by his wife, Mary Magdalene, the descendants of which, from the Merovingian Dynasty (476-760), formed the royal houses of Europe. What a better way to set up oneself as the true Messiah, and eventually announce that you are *the true incarnation of God.*

In March, 2007, an event came to pass which I had long been expecting.

Jewish film-maker Simcha Jacobvisa, in collaboration with Oscar-winning Hollywood director James Camron, of *Titanic* fame, released a $3.5 million dollar documentary called, *The Lost Tomb of Jesus,* a ninety-minute film, which first aired on the Discovery Channel in the U.S. on March 4.

This was accompanied by the release of Jacobvisi's book, *The Jesus Family Tomb: The Discovery, the Investigation, and the Evidence that Could Change History*, written with the aid of Charles Pellegrino, originator of the *Jurassic Park* DNA cloning concept. The idea that Pellegrino was involved emits thoughts of attempting the cloning of humans. Most shocking is the possibility of future claims to use this process on what might be crudely interpreted to be the remains of Jesus.

A striking dark implication which could lead to a demonic proclamation of a **second coming**! The idea has been thought of by some who have looked for ways to produce a king which could be said to be **Jesus himself**! My source is confidential, but real.

The film documents the discovery of the first century tomb containing several ossuaries, unearthed in 1980 during excavations in East Talpiot, a Jerusalem suburb, three miles to the east.

Ossuaries are rectangular shaped limestone bone boxes commonly used in the final stage of Jewish burial in the time of Christ. The procedure was to transfer the bones of the family members from the original tomb to an ossuary about one year after the initial burial.

The premise of the film was that the names on the boxes in this tomb matched members of the family of Jesus of Nazareth. Some of the ossuaries which are now identified as coming from the tomb were unmarked, but several had etchings indicating the name of the individual whose bones had been put to rest in them. One ossuary, the smallest and least significant, carried a dull etching, *Yehoshua bar Yehoseph*, in Aramaic, the language spoken by Jesus. The English interpretation of this is "Jesus, son of Joseph." Others were *Yos'*, or Joses, which could have been one of Jesus' brothers; *Marya*, Hebrew for Mary, *Matya*, a Hebrew form of Matthew (this person was not identifiable as a possible close family member), *Mariamme e Mora*, Greek meaning Mariam or Martha. This name, they claimed, was used in the Gnostic gospel of Phillip as that of Mary Magdalene. The final marked ossuary bore the inscription, *Jehuda bar Yehoshua*, the Hebrew equivalent of Judas, son of Joshua, or Jesus.

The film told the story of the effort of their crew to locate the original tomb, and of their success in doing so. It had been covered up beneath an apartment complex, and they took the liberty, without the permission of the authorities, to uncover it and descend into the actual tomb. They then found that it had originally held ten bone boxes, and that one of them had disappeared shortly after the dig. The missing box was later identified as the James ossuary which had surfaced previously, causing controversy among scholars worldwide. Part of the inscription had been proven to be a forgery.

Although, according to law, the bones from the ossuaries had been removed immediately after the original dig, the film-makers conveniently found residue which they believed might possibly belong to Jesus and Mary Magdalene.

The residue was taken to the DNA testing facility at Lakehead University in Thunder Bay, Ontario, Canada for analysis.

The laboratory allegedly found traces of human mtDNA, thereby concluding that the samples were of two different individuals from different mothers. It was stated that since they were from the same family tomb, the two were likely husband and wife! There was no mention that this could easily have been the wife of another individual in the tomb; in addition, there were no samples of others proving this supposed relationship.

When the original dig had been made, it had been listed as inconsequential. The names were simply too common in the first century.

The film was immediately attacked, not only by Christians, but equally by individuals having no belief in the resurrection of Jesus, such as Sir Lawrence Gardner (1943-2010), author of *Bloodline of the Holy Grail: The Hidden Lineage of Jesus Revealed*, 1996, and Professor Fida Hassnain (1924-2016), Sufi, author of *The Search for the Historical Jesus* which supports the legend that Jesus traveled to India after his crucifixion, which allegedly did not kill him; that he preached there and is buried in Srinagar.

There are many reasons why this film was ridiculous.

Though the authors took great pains to create a believable premise, it has been shown that they searched for a tomb which might fulfill the purpose of discrediting the resurrection of Jesus and give credence to the James ossuary. Archaeologists like William Dever, whom the Washington Post called, "an expert on near eastern archaeology and anthropology, who has worked with Israeli archaeologists for five decades," [3] even saw through their plot. And he's not a Christian, either. Christians strong in their faith naturally reject the obvious façade. Still, many agnostics believe this story, just as they did at the time of the Resurrection.

It seems ironic that the Discovery Channel's Tom Robinson did a 2006 special titled, *The Real Da Vinci Code,* in which he found the claims supported by Dan Brown to be totally unfounded; their basis formed upon a hoax. But the seeds are still being planted, and the public as a whole is hungry for spectacular scandals.

Brit-Am Israel, headed by a Jew in the nation of Israel, known as Yair Dividiy, has for many years proclaimed that the Jews should accept members of the 'lost tribes' from Europe as Israelites, and welcome them back to their true homeland. He publishes a magazine, puts out a newsletter, and has written several books on this subject. [4] The problem here is not the teaching that the lost tribes settled in Europe and Britain, but the fact that Jews may accept a powerful leader of the now-expanding **European Union** (EU) as the promised messiah.

This confederation of nations is getting set up to be the future ruling empire of the Western World, and may even be in league with the U.S. A confidential high-ranking source told me in *strict confidence* that the election of Donald Trump in 2016 was foreknown by the 'powers that be.' Whether this was genuine, I have no way of knowing. However, Romans 13:1b tells us:

"...there is no power but of God: the powers that be are ordained of God."

One strong leader emerging at present is French President Emanuel Macron, whose picture on the front of the weekly news magazine, *The Economist,* June 17, 2017, showed him walking on water. The publication declared him, "Europe's Next Savior." Is the name Emanuel a mere coincidence?

Macron was formally an investment banker with Rothschild and Cie Banque, now a member of the Rothschild Group which specializes in mergers and acquisitions. The Jewish Rothschild family is the premier banking family of France. Immediately prior to his election as French President, he served as Minister of Economy and Finance.

In 2018, he addressed the World Economic Forum in Davos, Switzerland. A Toi Staff article on October 21, 2018 in *The Times of Israel* was titled "Macron to Unveil Peace Plan Soon if Trump Doesn't, Top Diplomat Said to Tell MKs." The picture is of Macron shaking hands with smiling Palestinian Authority President, Mahmoud Abbas, in Paris on December 22, 2017. A second photo is of Macron with Israeli Prime Minister, Benjamin Netanyahu.

Of course nothing is 'set in stone.' However, it is evident that the world, much like first century Israel, is looking for a solid solution to the problems that, even now, loom on the horizon for the troubled world economy.

Leading economic indicators predict a crash as early as late this year. On December 10, 2018, the *New York Times* printed an article by Alex Williams titled, "Are You Ready for the Financial Crisis of 2019?" The article states that for most of the past year, the situation for "moneyed Americans has felt like 1929 all over again." Williams cites indicators as student loans, China, the end of easy money, Italexit (continuing problems in the European Union), and number one, an anti-billionaire uprising across America. Other such articles are not uncommon, with either 2019 or 2020 as the beginning of this collapse. Such an event could easily pave the way for a charismatic leader to step up with a solution.

The best-selling book by David Icke, *The Biggest Secret*, subtitled, *The Book that Will Change the World* (1998, Bridge of Love Publications, U.K.), is riddled with statements about the St. Clairs/Sinclairs, calling them "Black Nobility," [5] and placing them at the center of the global conspiracy of the New World Order. He also classifies us as members of an extraterrestrial "reptilian race," descending from the serpent who tempted Eve, who have controlled the world for thousands of years. [6]

This doctrine springs from the teaching that original sin was Eve's sexual union with the serpent, who was an alien from another planet.

As a Commissioner, later a Vice President of Clan Sinclair Association, U.S.A., I am proud to announce that most of our members do not believe these heresies, though some will undoubtedly get caught up in the excitement, as will various other well-meaning people.

As the co-founder of the worldwide St. Clair Research, and its YDNA project, in which many of our number have been tested, I can verify that the vast majority of us are of the Haplogroup R1b, not Mediterranean; the only bit of truth being the fact that our ancestors have been in Europe for thousands of years before Christ.

The reptilian race doctrine is utter nonsense. The serpent was none other than the spirit being whom we now know as 'the devil.' The original sin was disobedience to the Creator.

DNA evidence presented by Spencer Wells in *The Journey of Man* shows conclusively that all peoples descended from one man, whom Wells sees as coming from North Africa, [7] not far, indeed, from Mesopotamia, in which the biblical creation of Adam (man) is viewed as taking place.

I see our clan as a scapegoat for those who would set the stage for this delusion. When I was contacted by the *National Geographic Channel* for a possible television interview, I was quick to state that I would cooperate based on expressing my own views. Obviously the segment was cut, and the special went in a different direction.

Chapter Fifteen

Sign Number Eleven: Solar Eclipse Accompanied by a Meteor Shower

In the mythical story of Superman, his coming to earth was accompanied by a meteor shower, a fact that was played up in the television series *Smallville*, (2001-2011), first on WB, then CW network. The child, the son of a divine ruler of another planet, Krypton, which has been destroyed, is found in a small spaceship sent to earth by his father to do his bidding. The child, discovered by a farm family named Kent, is adopted by them. The Kents quickly realize that young Clark has super powers. Eventually, despite messages from his spirit-father, he finally decides that his mission on earth is to do good and fight evil.

In a distorted way, this character reminds us of the Son of God. His second appearing is preceded by a meteor shower and an eclipse of the sun. These signs in the heavens will appear suddenly; after all other prophecies have been fulfilled. In keeping, we can certainly say that Christ could then re-appear at any moment. In chapter one of this book, I mentioned the statement of Jesus to his disciples after he had revealed the remarkable signs which would appear before his second coming. He told them, "This generation will not pass till all these things be fulfilled." [1] Then he said, "heaven and earth shall pass away, but my words shall not pass away." [2]

What opponents of Christ's authority fail to see is that the two verses immediately preceding Christ's statement that this generation shall not pass before the prophecies are fulfilled are key to their timing:

"Now learn a parable of the fig tree: When his branch is yet tender, and putteth forth leaves, ye know that summer is nigh: So likewise ye, when ye shall see all these things know that the time is near, even at the doors." [3]

The fig tree in scripture is symbolic of the nation of Israel. In 1948, as mentioned earlier, Israel became a nation. The generation birthed at the time that Israel became a nation would be my own generation, as I was born in 1946. When a generation passes, it means it dies out. In scripture it states that up until the patriarchs, Abraham, Isaac and Jacob, men lived much longer lives. After that, the average human life is said to be seventy to eighty years. "And the days of our years are three score and ten years, and if by reason of strength they be fourscore years, yet is their strength labour and sorrow, for it is soon cut off and we fly away." [4]

In their Greek Lexicon, Arndt and Gingrich state that γενιάς στην (genea), translated generation in Matthew 24, refers generally to "the sum of years of those born at the same time, expanded to include all those living at a given time generation, contemporaries." [5]

Using today's life expectations, members of this generation will still be alive a bit longer than even this.

Chapter Sixteen

Final Sign, Number Twelve: Christ's Coming Will Be Immediately After the Tribulation

Fundamentalist churches, including those with whom I have been affiliated, have long preached the pre-tribulation return of the Christ to catch the Church away. Some groups, today, are seeing the error of this teaching. Churches which have taught this doctrine for so long would naturally be reluctant to admit that it may not hold water. No one who understands the situation wants to be on earth during this cataclysmic time. But there are problems with the pre-trib teaching which cannot be overlooked.

The first and most obvious problem with a pre-trib 'rapture' is that the event described in Matthew 24 mentioned earlier: "And He will send forth His angels **with a great trumpet and they will gather together His elect from the four winds**," [1] is after the tribulation. [2] This is a match with Paul's statement in his first epistle to the church in Corinth, which is attributed to the 'rapture:' "In a moment, in the twinkling of an eye, **at the last trump: for the trumpet shall sound, and the dead shall be raised**..." [3]

The gathering together of the saints at his coming, so clearly foretold by Christ as taking place after the tribulation, states that the **"elect" are gathered from the four winds**. Where are the "four winds," but all directions of the compass **on the earth**? A key here is "LAST TRUMP." If the 'rapture' takes place at the **"last trump**." and the gathering of the saints at the Second Coming, after the tribulation, is accompanied by a great trumpet, it is surely evident that these are one and the same event.

Much ado has been expressed over **when the signs in the heavens take place**.

Let's examine each of the scriptures which foretell this event, starting by re-reading Jesus' words from this all-important chapter of Matthew 24:

"But immediately <u>after the tribulation</u> of those days the sun will be darkened and the moon will not give her light, and the stars will fall from the sky, and the powers of the heavens will be shaken, and then the sign of the Son of Man will appear in the sky..." [4]

The following prophecy from the Old Testament book of Joel is repeated in the Acts of the Apostles:

"The sun shall be turned into darkness, and the moon into blood, before the great and terrible day of the Lord come." [5] [6]

And from the book of Revelation:

"And I beheld when he had opened the sixth seal, and, lo, there was a great earthquake; and the sun became black as sackcloth of hair, and the moon became as blood; And the stars of heaven fell into the earth, even as a fig tree casteth her untimely figs when she is shaken of a mighty wind. And the heaven departed as a scroll when it is rolled together; and every mountain and island were moved out of their places." [7]

These predictions all point to what seem to be the same event. Is it? Jesus said, without reservation, that after the tribulation there would be a darkening of the sun and moon. The stars would fall and the heavens would be shaken. Like many other events in the Bible, we know that these predictions may be attributed to natural phenomena.

As I brought out earlier, a solar eclipse, and a meteor shower could fulfill this prophecy. Jesus had said just prior to this that his coming would be "...as the lightening cometh out of the east and shineth unto the west..." [8] <u>He never said that he would return more than once.</u>

The scripture above from Joel 2, when taken in context, has to do with the "Day of the Lord," when God's spirit would be poured out on all flesh." In the very next verse, it says, "in Mount Zion and in Jerusalem shall be deliverance, as the Lord hath said, and in the remnant whom the Lord shall call."

Could the final conclusion of this be at the return of Messiah? In the passage from Acts, **immediately prior** to the quoting of the prophecy of the signs in the heavens, it states that the Day of Pentecost was in fulfillment of the prophecies of Joel, or that this obviously **BEGAN** their fulfillment. This will come into greater understanding in the **last chapter when I reveal my shocking conclusion**.

"But this is that which was spoken by the prophet Joel, And it shall come to pass in the last days, saith God, I will pour out of my Spirit upon all flesh: and your sons and daughters shall prophesy, and your young men shall see visions, and your old men shall dream dreams; And on my servants and on my handmaids I shall pour out in those days of my Spirit; and they shall prophesy: And I will show wonders in heaven above, and signs in the earth beneath; and fire and vapor of smoke." [9]

Obviously, the day of Pentecost was not the conclusion of the fulfillment of the end time prophecy of Joel. All of the natural phenomena have not come to pass; not even with the recent "four blood moons." But it was the beginning.

The prophecy from Revelation is very similar to these, but the placement of it in the order of the book of Revelation makes it too soon to be the signs which will accompany the return of Christ. Our world is shaken by the attempt of man to explore space. Since the Bible says that God was displeased with man for building the tower of Babel, [10] the intent of which was that its top *may reach* unto heaven," how much more is man stretching his limit by sending rockets, satellites, probes and a 'space station' into the heavens? If space exploration doesn't upset the balance of nature, as NASA seems to believe, why the drastic increase in natural disasters? Why are we experiencing global warming?

On November 9, 2006, a colossal hurricane-like storm appeared on Saturn [11] near its south pole. This was the first time such a storm had ever been known to develop on any planet other than earth. It was said to be much larger than our hurricanes; about 5,000 miles wide, and five times higher, with a well-defined eye, churning in a clockwise motion at 350 miles per hour. NASA scientists were baffled.

But what about his feet touching at the Second Coming? The 'rapture' scriptures don't say that. The Bible does not say that his feet will immediately touch the Mount of Olives when he comes. This is from Christian tradition, based on a verse in the writings of the prophet Zechariah regarding the Day of the Lord:

"And his feet shall stand in that day upon the mount of Olives, which is before Jerusalem on the east, and the mount of Olives shall cleave in the midst thereof toward the east and toward the west, and there shall be a very great valley; and half of the mountain shall remove toward the north, and half toward the south." [12]

The belief that his feet would touch down on the Mount of Olives was established due to tradition that this is where he ascended into the heavens. This also, is not found in canon scripture. Matthew and John do not even mention his ascension, and it is only briefly alluded to in Mark and Luke.

"So then after the Lord had spoken unto them, he was received up into heaven, and sat on the right hand of God." [13]

"And it came to pass, while he blessed them, he was parted from them, and carried up into heaven." [14]

The most detailed account of the ascension is found in the book of the Acts of the Apostles 1:9-11, also attributed to Luke:

"And when he had spoken these things, while they beheld, he was taken up; and a cloud received him out of their sight. And while they looked steadfastly toward heaven as he went up, behold, two men stood by them in white apparel: Which also said, Ye men of Galilee, why stand ye gazing up into heaven? This same Jesus, which is taken up from you into heaven, shall come in like manner as ye have seen him go into heaven."

But if the scriptures do not support the doctrine of the pre-tribulation rapture, where and when did this originate? The answer is simple. This doctrine was first taught by a minister of the Church of Scotland, Edward Irving, who was dismissed from his position for belief and practice of spiritual gifts, including speaking in tongues, in 1832.

Two years earlier, during one of Irving's services, a 15 year old Scottish girl named Margaret McDonald went into a 'trance.' After a period of several hours, in which she claimed to have a vision, she prophesied that Christ's coming would be in two phases, rather than one, as had been believed and taught by Christians up to this point. She said that Christ would come visibly to catch away only the righteous of all nations; then he would come a second time to pronounce judgment upon the unrighteous of all nations. [15] This 'secret rapture' doctrine was then promoted by Irving, who stated that he had heard a voice from heaven commanding him to proclaim this message. After Irving's dismissal from the Church of Scotland, he formed the Catholic Apostolic Church, which still exists today.

Later, Englishman John Darby, pioneer of the Plymouth Brethren movement, took hold of the rapture doctrine introduced by Irving, and went to Scotland to meet with him and his followers. Darby became the developer of the scriptural arguments which are still used to support it. But its inclusion by Cyrus Scofield in his *Scofield Reference Bible* made the pre-trib rapture spread throughout the world.

The scripture invariably used to support the rapture doctrine is found in the Apostle Paul's first epistle to the Thessalonian church.

After telling them that he would "not have (them) igno-rant...concerning them which are asleep" [16] (dead), Paul gives them assurance of a resurrection at "the coming of the Lord." [17]

"For the Lord himself shall descend from heaven with a shout, with the voice of the archangel, and with the **trump of God**; and the dead in Christ shall rise first; Then we which are alive and remain shall be caught up together with them in the clouds to meet the Lord in the air; and so shall we ever be with the Lord. But the times and the seasons, brethern, ye have no need that I write unto you. For yourselves know perfectly well that the Lord cometh as a thief in the night. For when they say, Peace and safety, then sudden destruction cometh upon them, as travail upon a woman with child; and they shall not escape. But ye, brethren, are not in darkness that that day should overtake you as a thief." [18]

By examining these scriptures we see that [1] Paul was not putting this in a time frame, simply stating what would happen **at the return of Christ**; [2] **In no way** did he state that this was a separate event from the 'Second Coming;' [3] This event could not be a secret mission in which the Christians would be caught away, because it was accompanied by **the sound of the trumpet**, exactly as Jesus stated his coming after the Tribulation would be; [4] The followers of Christ, whether living or dead, would meet Christ, just as Jesus said would happen in his coming after the Tribulation.

Also, after questions by the Thessalonian Christians concerning the event, in his next letter to them he said:

"Now we beseech you, brethren, by the coming of our Lord Jesus Christ, and by our gathering together with him, That ye be not soon shaken in mind, or be troubled, neither by spirit, nor by word, nor by letter as from us, as that the day of Christ is at hand. Let no man deceive you by any means; for that day shall not come except there be a falling away first, and that the man of sin be revealed, the son of perdition." [19]

Here Paul himself clarifies the fact that before the coming of the Lord, which he mentioned in his first letter, or epistle, to them, would not come until after the Tribulation when the "man of sin," aka the Anti-Christ, is revealed.

Chapter Seventeen

Hard Evidence

Let's recap the facts to this point which provide evidence that Christ will return soon.

First, Israel became a nation in 1948, setting the stage for end-time events to begin.

Second, never before in world history have the times all came together to be as Jesus said it would be. People are "running to and fro" and knowledge is being increased, [1] as Daniel predicted, like never before. Automobiles, trains and especially jets, have made this the greatest travel age in all of man's history. Computers and satellite television have made the information generation boom beyond anything before dreamed possible. The prophecies recorded in this passage which Daniel was to "shut up the words and seal the book, even to the time of the end," were never able to be understood before. Now they are making sense.

Third, the prophecies of Jesus in Matthew 24 could never have been fulfilled in any one generation until **NOW!** False messiahs and prophets have shown their ugly heads, wars are everywhere, natural disasters, including earthquakes, in "divers places" [2] are rampant, causing multiplied hundreds of thousands of deaths. Disaster teams are working around the clock, and around our sphere. The word 'tsunami' is now a household word.

Fourth, insulting the Christian faith in America, even within our generation, would have been a mouth-dropping event for most of us. Now it is common-place. Don't insult the religions of other nations, that might offend them, but in the twenty-first century it is considered normal to doubt the tenants of Christianity, and seek 'enlightenment' through gnosis and mystics. False prophets are having a hay day. There is truly a "falling away" by many, as churches who genuinely have faith in the Lordship of Christ experience a decline in membership, also in accord with prophecy, and abuse of children by Catholic priests and Prosperity Gospel zealots who have fallen from grace have made matters even worse.

Fifth, the other prophecies are set to be fulfilled. Wycliffe Bible Translators are pushing full speed ahead to have the Bible translated into every dialect on earth, so every person can hear the Gospel.

Sixth, the 'enlightenment' believers in the New Age are setting the stage for the acceptance of the Anti-Christ. One book promoting the arrival of the One World leader from the "line of Jesus" stated that "all the necessary conditions are now in place." [3] He sees this system as bringing about "heaven on earth." [4] **The fact that the system is poised for the proper moment, is compelling evidence that the prophets in the Bible had divine foreknowledge of this day in which we are living.**

The stage is surely set for Armageddon.

Many have been so convinced that the hour was upon us that they have misread the signs, and felt that the catching away of God's "elect" should have happened around the year 2,000. **Why were they wrong? If we are this close, why haven't the other prophecies already been fulfilled?** If even the New Age Movement was pushing for their leader to come on the scene, why has it not happened? **My shocking conclusion is just ahead**.

My Shocking Theory

Whenever the current church age is mentioned, it has always
been presumed to have begun at the birth of Jesus. The
following excerpt from my book, *Prayers of Prophets, Knights
and Kings*, includes the first step to understanding where we
are in the scheme of prophecy, and why so many were wrong
in setting dates for the return of Christ:

*"At the time of the birth of Christ Zoroastrianism was the
prevailing religion in Persia, and Babylonia. The Magi were
'wise men' who were advisors to the kings. They followed the
teaching of Zarathustra, and were accomplished astronomers,
and believed in a prophecy that God was going to send a
messiah, or anointed one. According to a 2002 BBC special,
'The Mystery of the Three Kings', a sign in the stars was to
announce his birth. Since the reign of Roman puppet king
Herod the Great, during which Jesus was stated to be born
was only from 8 BC to 4 BC, the traditional birth date for Jesus
is obviously inaccurate. The most likely date, according to the
BBC special, was April 16, 6 BC (13 Sh'vat) when Jupiter was
in the Eastern sky and eclipsed with the moon, rather than a
comet or supernova as some have believed.*

*"According to BBC, astronomer Michael Molnor of Rutgers
University has discovered an ancient coin from around the time
of Jesus birth, depicting Aries, the ram, jumping, looking back
at a star. The clue led to documents revealing that Judea was
frequently depicted under the sign of Aries. Astrological events
around this time showed one significant event; that mentioned
above. To the Magi, this could likely have been a sign of the
birth of the Messiah."* [1]

This shows one very possible date for the birth of Jesus. He
was certainly not born on December 25th, a date set by
Constantine in 360 AD to coincide with a pagan holiday,
celebrated as the birth of the sun god, which was already

being observed at the time when he made Christianity the official religion of the Roman Empire.

After my long believing April 16/17 to be the correct date for Jesus birth, another interesting theory came to my attention in an article by a modern researcher titled, "Historical Dates for Jesus Christ." It uses the time of Mary's most probable conception based on the text found in Luke's gospel when Mary was visited by the angel:

"And in the sixth month the angel Gabriel was sent from God unto a city of Galilee named Nazareth, To a virgin espoused to a man whose name was Joseph, of the house of David, and the virgin's name was Mary." [2]

The sixth month of the Hebrew religious calendar was the month of Adar, from the Akkadian *Adaur,* (February/March). At that time Elizabeth had already been pregnant with John for six months. Some believe this meant the sixth month of Elizabeth's pregnancy, but it doesn't say so. Without going into elaborate detail, because of the office and duties of John the Baptist's father, Zachariah; the timing of the angel Gabriel's visit to Mary, and the time of Herod; the researcher arrived at a birth date of Tishri 15, or October 8, 7 BC. [3] My problem with this date was that I had seen no evidence that a conjunction of stars had occurred around that time which would qualify this possible date to be considered. After finding out the depth of study which this researcher had undergone to derive at this date, I dug further.

First, I found out that in 1603, Dutch astronomer and mathematician Johannes Kepler became the first to observe a conjunction between the planets Jupiter and Saturn in the Constellation Pisces, noting that by their converging, they appeared as a larger and new 'star.' [4]

Later, Kepler remembered having read the writings of Abravanel, [5] a brilliant Portuguese rabbi who lived from 1436 to 1508, in which he stated that Jewish astronomers believed that when there was a conjunction of Jupiter and Saturn, the Messiah would come.

In 1925, this hypothesis was reexamined when references to this conjunction were discovered in the cuneiform inscriptions of the archives of the ancient Babylonian School of Astrology in Sipper. This conjunction had been recorded over a period of five months in 7 BC. Calculations show that this bright 'star' was visible three times over the course of that year: May 29, **October 3**, and December 4! [6]

At this point I felt that there was real validity in this time frame. The Persian Magi would have been aware of this. I felt that this researcher could have been off by a few days and still plausible in his theory. Another fascinating fact was that October 3, 7 BC was Saturday, Tishri 10, 3755 on the Jewish calendar, the **Day of Atonement**! Given Mary's probable date of divine conception, this birth would have been slightly premature, but with the journey to Bethlehem on a donkey, this makes a lot of sense.

But was Jesus' birth actually the date when the church age began? In the book of the Acts of the Apostles, we find **the undisputed birth of the church was on the Day of Pentecost**, as I mentioned earlier in chapter fifteen. **This point is the final key**.

After I pondered this thought, it became clear to me that **the measurement of time until the end of the age began after the end of Christ's earthly ministry, not at his birth**!

Several dates have been calculated for the crucifixion of Christ, the first being set by Sir Isaac Newton, using the visibility of the crescent moon in order to correlate the Judean and Julian calendars. His preferred date was Friday April 23, 34 AD. The most commonly accepted dates by researchers today are Friday April 7, 30 AD and Friday April 3, 33 AD, [7] but generally, these researchers assumed Jesus birth at the beginning of the Gregorian calendar AD and his age 33 at his death. However, according to the prophecies which we have already reviewed in Daniel, the time is most certain that the Messiah would be revealed.

Some have seen this as when he began his ministry. But that was not the date on which he showed himself to be the Messiah. **Upon his triumphal entry, when he rode into Jerusalem on the donkey, he truly showed himself to be Messiah**.

Peter and Paul La Londe, in *301 Startling Proofs and Prophecies* (Prophecy Partners, Inc., Niagara Falls, Ontario, Canada, 1996) state that 483 years later, to the day, was Sunday, April 6, 32 AD, and that this coincides with the commemoration of Palm Sunday on which Jesus rode into Jerusalem, revealing himself to be the Messiah. Only days later, the prophecy of his slaying was also fulfilled.

This date, however, did not ring as accurate for two reasons. First, since there was no year 0, and 465 BC was the first year of Artaxerxes' reign over Media and Persia, the twentieth year of his reign would have been 446 BC. Thus, 483 years from 446 BC, it seemed, would have been 37 AD, or 3797 of the Hebrew calendar, [8] not 32 AD. Secondly, Jesus met with his disciples to eat the Seder meal the night of his arrest. This was only celebrated on the first night of Passover in Judea, which is normally Nisan 14. In 32 AD, Nisan 14 was on Monday. [9] Though most Christians consider this to have been on Thursday, and the crucifixion on Friday, when I pondered the idea that the day of crucifixion was a "high day," not a regular Sabbath, it began to make sense that the crucifixion was on Wednesday, as others have suggested, and the high day was on Thursday. This will be covered later, but the clincher definitely came when I found out that the only years that fell this way around that time were 3787 and 3797! I was shocked again!

The first discovery is that the *likely* date of Jesus' birth was October 3, 7 BC, in Tishri, the Day of Atonement. His revelation as Messiah, and his crucifixion and resurrection all being in Nisan. If this was 37 AD, according to Daniel's prophecy, this would have made him forty-three years of age, not thirty-three, when his ministry of three years began.

I had originally felt that the birth of the church had been in 27 AD because of the signs which I had uncovered, or 3787 on the Jewish calendar. Evidence showed that Daniel's seventieth week was nearer.

The Gospel attributed to Luke, immediately after the baptism of Jesus, states, regarding his ministry:

"And Jesus began his ministry to be about thirty years of age." [10]

I was perplexed as to the prophecy of Daniel. The understanding of this is "from the going forth of the commandment to restore and build Jerusalem." [11]

The original decree to rebuild Jerusalem had been given by Cyrus much earlier, in the first year of his reign after taking Babylon, 538 BC. [12] According to Josephus, in *The Antiquities of the Jews*, Cyrus read in the book of Isaiah that he had been foretold to rebuild Jerusalem over 100 years earlier, and gave a decree for it to be done:

"This was known to Cyrus by reading the book which Isaiah left behind him of prophecies; for this prophet said that God had spoken it to him in a secret vision: 'My will is that Cyrus, whom I have appointed to be king over many nations, send back my people to their land and build their temple.'" [13]

The prophecy from Isaiah [14] is one of the most convincing prophecies in the Bible. The fulfillment is found in the Bible in both II Chronicles [15] and Ezra. [16]

The work which had begun in Jerusalem had been ceased when the people complained, and an order had been given by Artaxerxes recorded by Ezra:

"Give ye now commandment to cause these men to cease, and that this city be builded, until another commandment shall be given from me." [17]

The work on the Temple did not proceed until the second year of Darias [18] (520-519 BC), and in 457 BC or 3304 on the Jewish calendar (**the seventh year of his reign**), after the temple was complete, Artaxerxes wrote a letter, issuing an edict or 'commandment' [19] for Ezra to return to Jerusalem, establish a priesthood, and set up the government there.

This, in effect, would rebuild the city of Jerusalem, and was **the going forth**! This happened on the first of Nisan when Ezra left, or March 26. From this decree of Nisan 1, 3304, adding 483 years, and remembering that there is no year 0, it equals the very year that I had originally figured for the crucifixion, 3787, or **27 AD**!

The preparation of the Passover was always the day before the Sedar meal, and this is Nisan 14, beginning **on the evening of the 13th**. In 27 AD, Nisan 14 fell on Wednesday. The sign of the prophet Jonah was the only sign that Jesus gave to prove his true mission when questioned in Matthew's gospel by the scribes and Pharisees:

"An evil and adulterous generation seeks for a sign; but no sign shall be given it except the sign of the prophet Jonah. **For as Jonah was three days and three nights in the belly of the whale, so will the Son of Man be three days and three nights in the heart of the earth**. The men of Nineveh will rise at the judgment with this generation and condemn it; for they repented at the preaching of Jonah, and behold, something greater than Jonah is here. The Queen of the South will arise at the judgment with this generation to condemn it, and behold, something greater than Solomon is here." [20]

This scene is also recorded in Luke, and another reference is also given in Matthew.

Figuring in a Friday crucifixion, there is **no way** to fulfill this imperative prophecy of Jesus. Three days and three nights could only be completed by a Wednesday crucifixion.

It is obvious that Jesus, knowing the hour had come, met with the disciples secretly on Tuesday evening, which was the first evening of Passover since the Jewish day began at sunset, to observe his Paschal Sedar. Since the triumphal entry enraged the Jews so much, they were desperate to find him. It had likely only been two days between his triumphal entry on Sunday, and his arrest on Tuesday night after their 'Last Supper.'

Now it all fits. Crucifixion on Wednesday before the "high day," at a time when the Passover was beginning, makes sense. The day after the crucifixion was no ordinary Sabbath. It couldn't have been for the prophecy to be fulfilled which Jesus proclaimed as <u>the only sign which he would give to show that his claims were true</u>!

In the book of Leviticus, when the feasts were set up, the day following the Feast of the Passover was the Feast of Unleavened Bread, [21] **a 'high day.'** Thursday, Friday and Saturday were three days. Wednesday night, Thursday night and Friday night were three nights. Nowhere do the scriptures proclaim that he was in the grave all of Saturday night. Very early on the morning of the first day of the week, he had already arisen!

By his crucifixion on Nisan 14, he fulfilled for the believer in him the eternal pass-over from death to life.

In the words of the Apostle Paul, formerly the vile persecutor of Christians, Saul of Tarsus, "*For even Christ our Passover is sacrificed for us.*" (I Corinthians 5:7b)

Though the thoughts which pointed me in this direction are but re-workings of ongoing research, they would lead me to my unique theory, which I have never heard expressed before: **the belief that the beginning of the Christian Era, *thus the pivotal point in the understanding of the biblical prophecies of the end of the age,* began then**.

The birth of the church at Pentecost would have been **Sunday, Sivan 1, 27 AD, May 23**, according to our calendar. [22] 2,000 years from the date of the birth of the church, by this calculation, would be **May 23, 2027** (a Sunday). But from the Julian calendar, which was in use in the Roman Empire in the time of Christ, to the present Gregorian calendar, the time in years remained the same.

Of course we are not assured of dates, and <u>no one knows the day or the hour of his appearing</u>, so I can't claim to know that, but nowhere does the scripture state that we cannot know the approximate time! In fact, it ***strongly implies* that in the last days <u>we could know this</u>**. This would make the likely year for setting up the One World Government under the Anti-Christ **2020**.

When I settled on this theory, back in 2007, I decided to check **plans in the works for 2020**. I was amazed to find, even that early in the scheme of things, not only from religious organizations trying to prove the existence of the Illuminati, or one conspiracy theory or another, but from organizations or individuals who were genuinely expecting a major change around that same year.

Here are my early discoveries:

A great number of groups had already accepted the name 'Vision 2020.' Interestingly, 2020 is a symbol most recognized to represent <u>clear vision</u> by optometrists. The goal of New Age groups is **'enlightenment.'** The purpose of 'gnosis' is obtaining secret knowledge which will make us clearly see and understand deep occult 'mysteries.' In I Timothy 6:20b, Paul admonishes young Timothy: "Turn away from godless chatter and opposing ideas of what is falsely called knowledge." The Greek word here translated knowledge is *gnosis.*

The Anti-Christ will be a visionary leader, one who will personify knowledge, and claim to have all the answers.

He will have a plan for immediate world peace. The Middle East will finally sign a peace treaty, and the environment will receive great priority. Fuel will be affordable, and all people will be able to receive food and medical treatment. Sound good? From the present circumstances, as revealed in chapter fourteen, it is easy to see how this could even now quickly occur. Those who oppose the system once it is in place will need to be quietly eliminated.

Organizations in the U.S. and several other countries are known as Vision 2020. Apart from a worldwide initiative to the "Right to Sight," there are many other goals of these organizations, such as infrastructure and technology. Texas A & M University; the State of Illinois; Moscow, Idaho; Saginaw County Michigan; Joplin, Missouri; Bakersfield, California, and the U.S. chemical industry are among those who set up Vision 2020 programs early in this century, promoting excellence in the future. India 2020 Organization envisions a reduction of poverty, and better education and technology in their country.

One of the most notable and least known of these organizations is called *Fishnet*. No doubt these people are well-meaning. In part, their project, headquartered in New Zealand, sees for Vision 2020: "A possible future for humanity: wealth, sustainability, peace, adventure." This vision offers to create a base level of wealth that is equivalent to what a current U.S. citizen would call "high middle income." Of course, 2020 is almost here, and much is lacking yet, but the website promoting its goals is still active in 2019. [23] Some goals still listed are:

"This project will deliver everyone a home, food, education, communication and travel.

"It empowers personal responsibility by providing security and opportunity.

"We create a set of robots that can do all this and make another one for us.

"For those of you who doubt it is economically possible consider this:

"Having a machine that can do all aspects of production means it does so at no cost.

"This is a fundamental change to the structure of economic theory.

"The wealth created by this gives us the means to tackle all of the major ecological issues facing humanity, and to create whatever we responsibly choose."

Although this project alone has not yet been able to accomplish these goals, many groups continue toward major changes quickly. Ted Howard, organizer of Vision 2020 in New Zealand, is only one politician who may be swept aboard the New World Order, which is moving with all due diligence toward fulfillment of the prophecies of Jesus.

Whether the actual time is 2020 or not, it is drawing dreadfully near for these prophecies to come to pass.

According to a March 2006 broadcast in English on N.C.P. and C.P.P.C. Television, China had reportedly announced that they were working toward a better society, with greater human rights, and better acceptance of their ideals the world over. There target year, the report stated, is 2020. Truly, 2020 is a year when people around the world will be expecting new vision.

Then there is the goal of Wycliffe Bible Translators to complete the printing of the Bible in all languages by **2025**!

Is this a mere coincidence? Evangelical television ministries are beaming their messages into almost every corner of the world already.

Then I started looking at 2025. If my theory holds true, by late 2023 to early 2024, "the man of sin" should claim himself to be the incarnation of God. In Mark Palmer's futuristic novel, *Breaking the Real Axis of Evil*, the target date for freeing the world of all dictatorships and tyrannies is 2025, thus, according to the book, **bringing peace to earth**! [24]

A website titled 'Goddess Ascending' gives a timeline for Goddess Peace, which culminates in (guess when), "gently replacing the god of the father with the god of the mother by 2025." [25] New Age philosophy embraces the "divine feminine." Mary Magdalene's proclaimed union with Jesus has ignited a cult which has culminated in worship of her as a goddess.

Alouph Haroven, former Mossad member, and Director of the Human Dignity Program at Sikkuy, the Association for the Advancement of Civic Equality, in Jerusalem, put it like this:

"...**by the year 2025 peace between Palestinians and Israelis should facilitate the fulfillment of the vision of peace** offered by Prince Abdullah of Saudi Arabia, a comprehensive peace between Israel and all her Arab neighbors; peace not only as the end of wars, but also as the development of human relations between Arabs and Israelis in fields of shared interest, on an equal basis." [26]

Yossi Alpher, a consultant on Israeli-related issues, and co-editor of an Internet site wrote in *A Tense Peace* in 2002:

"It is reasonable to assume that within 10 years at the most, there will be a Palestinian state in nearly all of the West Bank and Gaza, with the Quds (East Jerusalem) as its capitol. **It will have signed a peace treaty with Israel. By 2025 all remnants of Israeli settlements built inside what becomes the sovereign territory of Palestine will have disappeared**. And a broad program for the resettlement and rehabilitation of the 1948 refugees and their descendants will be well underway." [27]

Although this did not happen by the time Alpher predicted, conditions are ripe for fulfillment in the near future, especially with both Macros and Trump intent on seeing peace in the region, and with both two state and one state solutions possible.

John, in Revelation 13, forecasts the days of the beast and the false prophet, equated with the 'end-time' prophecies of Jesus and Daniel. He speaks of an image being made of the beast:

"And he had power to give life unto the image of the beast, that the image of the beast should both speak, and cause that as many as would not worship the image of the beast should be killed.

"And he causeth all, both small and great, rich and poor, free and bond, to receive a mark in their right hand, or in their foreheads:

"And that no man might buy or sell, save he that had the mark, or the name of the beast, or the number of his name.

"Here is wisdom. Let him that hath understanding count the number of the beast: for it is the number of a man; and his number is Six hundred threescore and six." [28]

Much difference of belief has existed as to what the 'mark of the beast' might be, but it has become commonly accepted among fundamentalist theologians that this mark is one which may be read by a scanner, and which is recognized by a world computer bank. Numbers for identification have been prevalent in the U.S. for several decades through the Social Security system. Now, computers are used for keeping track of everything and everyone. Identity theft and online hacking are ever-growing concerns in the twenty-first century around the world. Electronic devices have been able to speak for many years. Except for 'burners,' cell phones must now be trackable.

The 'big brother' theory put forth by George Orwell in his remarkable work, *1984*, though not possible then, is very plausible now, and will be certain to be the order of the day when "computers will have more computing power than human brains." [29]

According to an article by Yohan John, Ph.D., in *Forbes*, March 2, 2016, *'How Powerful Is the Human Brain Compared to a Computer,'* which first appeared online on *Quora,* though in some ways our brains are still superior:

"...computers are more powerful that humans when it comes to executing simple step-by-step instructions."

2020 *could* certainly be the year that the false peace will come. When Jesus said "But of that day and hour knoweth no one, not even the angels of heaven, neither the Son, but the Father," [30] he did not say that in the end, we could not discern the closeness of time, nor that in the end, when the words of the book would be unsealed, we could not have knowledge of the Truth.

"But thou, O Daniel, shut up the words, and seal the book, even to the time of the end: many shall run to and fro, and knowledge shall be increased." [31]

When an area wide peace treaty is signed in the Middle East, beware. As Paul told the Thessalonians, "For when they shall say, Peace and safety, then sudden destruction cometh, upon them, as travail upon a woman with child; and they shall not escape." [32]

But there is hope. The very next verses read:

"But ye, brethren, are not in darkness, that that day should overtake you as a thief. Ye are children of light, and children of the day; we are not of the night, nor of darkness. Therefore let us not sleep, as *do* others, but let us watch and be sober."

Imagine the implications of the imagery involved in the saga of **Yeshua Messiah**, **Jesus the King**. Would it be difficult to believe that he was born on the Day of Atonement, symbolizing his atonement for the sins of mankind, crucified on the Passover, as the final sacrifice, and that he *may even* return on the Day of Pentecost, when the eternal Kingdom of God, of which the Church is the type, will begin, to never end?

Our hope is in our faith. Our faith is in the knowledge of the Truth.

Chapter One

1. White Buffalo Calf Woman Has Returned article http://adishakti.org/prophecies/23_white_buffalo_calf _woman_has_returned.htm
2. Malachi 4:1, II Peter 3:7,10
3. *Signs of Qiyamah*, Mohammed Ali Abu Zuhair Ali, Islamic Book Service, New Deli, India, 2000
4. Ibid, number 1
5. British Broadcasting Corporation website; bbc.co.uk
6. *World Weekly News*, New York, NY, U.S.A., July 29, 1997
7. Armageddon Online, www.armageddononline.org
8. The Holy Lance ("Spear of Destiny") and the Power to Rule the World, K.C. Blau http://www.kcblau.com/holylance/
9. Ibid.
10. The Date Setter's Diary, Todd Strandberg, http://www.raptureready1.com/rr-date-setters.html
11. *The Talmud*, tractate Avodah Zarah, p 9.
12. Matthew 16:28
13. Mark 9:1
14. Matthew 17:1-9, Mark 9:2-10, Luke 9:28
15. Matthew 17:1b-2

Chapter Two

1. Genesis 22:18
2. Genesis 17:21
3. Genesis 35:10-12
4. Numbers 24:37
5. Micah 5:2
6. Isaiah 7:14

7. Malachi 3:1
8. Psalm 118:26
9. Daniel 9:26
10. Zechariah 14
11. Haggai 2:7-9
12. Isaiah 40:3
13. Malachi 3:1
14. Daniel 9:24-26a, *Tanakh*, 1917 translation
15. *Nelson's Illustrated Bible Dictionary*, p 380 ©1986, Thomas Nelson Publications, Nashville, TN, U.S.A.
16. Nehemiah 2:1
17. *301 Startling Proofs and Prophecies*, Peter and Paul La Londe, Prophecy Partners, Inc., Niagara Falls, Ontario, Canada, 1996
18. Zechariah 9:9
19. Psalm 41:9
20. Zechariah 11:12, 13
21. Isaiah 50:6
22. Isaiah 53:12
23. Isaiah 53:5
24. Isaiah 53:7
25. Psalm 22:18
26. Zechariah 9:9
27. Archives: biblequestions.org, Holly Street Church of Christ, Denver, CO, U.S.A.

Chapter Three

1. The Tanakh, 1917 translation, Psalm 2:1-9
2. The Tanakh, 1917 translation, Numbers 24:17
3. I Corinthians 2:14
4. Revelation 5:5
5. Matthew 26:39
6. *Foxes Book of Martyrs*, John Foxe, 1516-1585, English translation, John Day, London, England,1563
7. John 1:1

8. John 20:28
9. John 17:5
10. Matthew 28:18
11. Hebrews 1:3
12. Hebrews 1:8

Chapter Four

1. Daniel 12:11
2. Matthew 24:1-31

Chapter Five

1. Isaiah 55:8
2. *Ten False Messiahs*, Wayne Simpson, Biblical Research Foundation, © 2000, permission to copy with copyright intact (2007)
3. Ibid, 2

Chapter Six

1. *The Century of Warfare*, Nexus-Martin Productions, Ltd., A&E Television Network, London, U.K, 1993

Chapter Seven

1. *Scarcity and Poor Relief in Eighteenth Century Ireland, the Subsistence Crisis of 1782-'84*, James Kelly, Irish Historical Studies, Vol. 28, (109), 1992
2. *The Great Calamity*, Christine Kinealy, Gill & Macmillan, New York, NY, U.S.A., 1992
3. ArtUkraine.com
4. Kyodo World News Service: Dateline Kobe, Japan, January 17, 2005 (Independent Japanese Service)
5. Killer Waves, *National Journal*, Washington, DC, U.S.A., October 29, 2005

6. Kyodo World News Service: Dateline Beijing, China. January 5, 2006
7. NBC Evening News, Friday, January 27, 2006
8. *Facts for Failures: Katrina Impact*, Allison Plyer, Published August 26, 2016 https://www.datacenterresearch.org/data-resources/katrina/facts-for-impact/
9. CBS., Is Global Warming Fueling Hurricanes? http://cbs.com/topstories/local_story_2405858
10. *Economist Magazine*, https://www.economist.com/middle-east-and-africa/2017/03/30/famine-menaces-20m-people-in-africa-and-yemen
11. Agence France Presse, Paris, France, October 8, 2005
12. CNN, Sunday October 9, 2005
13. Wikipedia article, Pestilence
14. WebMD, Frequently Asked Questions about Bird Flu https://www.webmd.com/cold-and-flu/flu-guide/what-know-about-bird-flu#1

Chapter Nine

1. Waco: The Inside Story, PBS
2. Daniel 12:12
3. David Koresh aka Vernon Wayne Howell (1959-1993) https://www.ancestry.com/boards/topics.obits/1085 75/mb.ashx
4. The Strongest Poison, Mark Lane, pp 199-206, Hawthorn, New York, NY, U.S.A., 1982
5. Newsweek Web Exclusive, *He Calls Himself God*, 2007
6. https://www.newsweek.com/he-calls-himself-god-103137
7. Are We Becoming a Godless Society? Editorial, Dr. Creflo A. Dollar, ©World Changers Church International
8. www.godlesshouston.com

Chapter Eleven

1. *A Carnival of Revolution, Central Europe, 1989*, p2, Kenney Padriac; Princeton University Press, Princeton, NJ, U.S.A., 2002
2. *Eastern Europe in the Twentieth Century and After*, R.J. Crampton, Routledge, Abington-On-Thames, U.K., 1997
3. Wycliffe Bible Translators, U.S.A
   https://www.wycliffe.org.uk/about/our-impact/

Chapter Twelve

1. Matthew 24:15-18
2. *Catholic Encyclopedia*, article, Abomination of Desolation
3. *New York Times*, Lander, Mark, Trump Recognizes Jerusalem as Israel's Capital and Orders U.S. Embassy to Move, Dec. 6, 2017
4. *New York Times*, Jeffress, Robert, Pastor Who Said Jews are Going to Hell Led Prayer at Jerusalem Embassy, May 14, 2018
5. America's Hidden Role in Hamas' Rise to Power, Stephen Zunes (2009, 2011)
   https://www.huffingtonpost.com/stephen-zunes/americas-hidden-role-in-h_b_155087.html
6. *The New York Times*, July 16, 2006
7. *Strong's Exhaustive Concordance of the Bible,* Greek Dictionary of the New Testament, James Strong, S.T.D., L.L.D., Abingdon Press, New York, NY, U.S.A, 1894, 1967
8. II Thessalonians 2:3,4
9. I John 2:18,22; I John 4:3; II John 1:7
10. I John 2:18
11. II Thessalonians 2:3
12. Revelation 19:20

13. II Thessalonians 2:3,4
14. *Breaking Israel News*: Record Setting Crowd at Passover Sacrifice Reenactment. Adam Eliyahu Berkowitz https://www.breakingisraelnews.com/66076/passover-sacrifice-makes-comeback-overlooking-temple-mount-photos/

Chapter Thirteen

1. Daniel 12:7
2. Revelation 6:11
3. Genesis 41:15-22
4. Matthew 24:24
5. Daniel 12:11
6. Daniel 9:13
7. Revelation 8:7-12
8. Matthew 24:22

Chapter Fourteen

1. *Holy Blood, Holy Grail*, ©1983; Baigent, Lincoln, and Leigh; Corgi, London, U.K., chapter 12 and after
2. *The Messianic Legacy*, Baigent, Lincoln, and Leigh, ©1986, Dell Publishing, New York, NY, U.S.A.
3. *The Washington Post*, article, "Documentary Shows Possible Jesus Tomb", Karen Matthews; Washington, DC, U.S.A., March 14, 2007
4. Website www.geocities.com/hiberi/
5. *The Biggest Secret*, David Icke, p 130; ©1999; Bridge of Love, London, U.K.
6. Ibid.
7. The Journey of Man, a Genetic Odyssey, National Geographic/ PBS Television Special, Spencer Wells, ©2002

Chapter Fifteen

1. Matthew 24:34b
2. Matthew 24:35
3. Matthew 24:32-33
4. Psalm 89:10
5. *A Greek Lexicon of the New Testament*, W.F Arndt & F.W. Gingrich, p 153, University of Chicago Press, Chicago, IL, U.S.A., 1957

Chapter Sixteen

1. Matthew 24:31
2. Matthew 24:29 (See also Mark 13:24, Luke 21:25)
3. I Corinthians 15:52a,b
4. Matthew 24:29, 30a
5. Joel 2:31
6. Acts 2:20
7. Revelation 6:12-14
8. Matthew 24:27a
9. Acts 2:16-19
10. Genesis 11:4-9
11. Reuters release, Thursday, November 9, 2006
12. Zechariah 14:4
13. Mark 16:19
14. Luke 24:51
15. *The Unbelievable Pre-Trib Origin*, Dave Mac Pherson, Heart of America Bible Society, U.S.A., ©1973
16. I Thessalonians 4:13a,b
17. I Thessalonians 15b
18. I Thessalonians 4:16-18, 5:1-4
19. II Thessalonians 2:1-3

Chapter Seventeen

1. Daniel 12:4

2. Matthew 24:7c
3. *Rex Deus*, p 286, Marilyn Hopkins, Tim Wallace Murphy, Graham Simmans; Element Books, Ltd., Shafresbury, Dorset, U.K., ©2000
4. Ibid, p 290.

Chapter Eighteen

1. *Prayers of Prophets, Knights and Kings*, p 136, Stanley J. St. Clair; Trafford Publishing Co., Victoria, BC, Canada, © 2006
2. Luke 1:26,27
3. Bill Bonnett, www.abdocate.net/dates.aspx
4. Follw the Star, www.ibiblo.org/bgreek/archives
5. JewishEncyclopedia.com, article, Aravanel
6. *History of the New Testament*, Jack Kilmon www.historian.net/NTHX.html
7. *The Magi and the Star*, Simo Parpola; Bible Archaeology Society; Bible Review, December, 2001, pp 16-23; 52 & 54
8. Hebrew Date Converter, hebcal.com/converter
9. The case for Thursday Crucifixion, Dr. Earnest L. Martin, Ph. D., ©May, 2001 www.askeim.com/n010501
10. Luke 3:23a
11. Daniel 9:25b
12. Abdicate-Historic Dates for Jesus Christ, www.abdocate.net/dates.aspx
13. *The Antiquities of the Jews*, Book 11, chapter one, division two; Josephus, first century AD
14. Isaiah 44:28
15. II Chronicles 36:21-23
16. Ezra 1:1-3
17. Ezra 4:21

18. *Keil and Delitzsch Commentary on the Old Testament*, Carl F. Keil, Franz Delitzsch, pp 23, 24; German, English translation, Edinburgh, Scotland, U.K.,1866
19. Ezra 4:21
20. Matthew 12:39-42
21. Leviticus 23:6
22. Calendar Stats, www.abdocate.net/dates/aspx Bill Bonnett
23. Vision 2020, New Zealand
   http://www.fishnet.co.nz/v2020/
24. *Breaking the Real Axis of Evil*, Mark Palmer, Rowman & Littlefield, New York, NY, U.S.A., 2005
25. Radical Goddess Theology,
   http://godmotherascending.blogspot.com/2005/08/goddesspeace-timeline_05.html
26. An Israeli View, Why a Shared Vision is Necessary, Alouph Hareven,
   www.bitterlemons.org/previous/bl250302ed11.html
27. An Israeli View, A Tense Peace, Yossi Alpher
   www.bitterlemons.org/previous/bl250302ed11.html
28. Revelation 13:15-18
29. *Journal of Evolution and Technology*, "When Will Computer Technology Match the Human Brain?" Hans Moravec, 1998
30. Matthew 24:36
31. Daniel 12:4
32. I Thessalonians 5:3
33. I Thessalonians 5:4-6

NOTES

NOTES

NOTES

www.ingramcontent.com/pod-product-compliance
Lightning Source LLC
Chambersburg PA
CBHW021935040426
42448CB00008B/1083